REAL WORLD LIFE SKILLS FOR YOUNG ADULTS

NAVIGATE CAREER SUCCESS, ESTABLISH FINANCIAL FREEDOM, DEVELOP ESSENTIAL SKILLS, GROW HEALTHY RELATIONSHIPS, FOSTER A GROWTH MINDSET & BUILD PHYSICAL WELL-BEING

ANDYN N. DANG

DEDICATION

This book is dedicated to my daughter Jessica and my son Hieuson, two young adults who are now stepping into an adulting journey. Your independence, determination, and intelligence are qualities that I am so proud of. I believe in your potential to achieve great things. Life is a journey of self-discovery, constant learning, determination to grow, and sharing. Do your best to accomplish all you set out to do, and remember to find joy and meaning every step of the way. I wish you both a future filled with endless possibilities, successes, and happiness. I am bursting with pride for you both.

June 2024
Love Dad

TABLE OF CONTENTS

INTRODUCTION

Arriving at the young adulthood stage in your life is like standing at the edge of a vast, uncharted territory: It's thrilling—full of potential, yet undeniably daunting! You're at a pivotal juncture in life where the decisions you make and the skills you acquire will set the trajectory for your future. This stage is brimming with opportunities to shape your destiny but also comes with its fair share of hurdles. It's a time when the need for guidance is most acute, yet the path to finding good and relevant guidance can often seem relatively obscure.

This is where my journey intersects with yours. My passion for empowering young adults like you to navigate this critical phase of life is the heart and soul of this book. With a blend of warmth and insightful wisdom, I aim to be the wise buddy you can rely on—a source of reputable, easy-to-follow guidance that resonates with your particular challenges and aspirations. My commitment to you is rooted in a deep understanding of the challenges faced in young adulthood, having navigated them myself and emerged with valuable lessons to share.

Real-World Life Skills for Young Adults is more than just a book; it's a comprehensive roadmap designed to guide you through the complexities of career-building, financial independence, and the mastery of essential life skills. It will help you enhance your time management and productivity while nurturing your mental and emotional well-being through self-reflection and personal growth. Our conversations will be candid, often humorous, and always empathetic, aiming to spark your curiosity and inspire action.

In today's fast-paced world, the gap in traditional education regarding practical life skills is more evident than ever. Through anecdotes, statistics, and real-life examples, we'll explore the essential skills that every young adult should possess—skills that are often overlooked. This book offers a beacon of hope and a wealth of knowledge to those willing to take the first steps toward self-reliance and personal fulfillment.

This book is structured to take you on a journey from setting off on your career path and mastering your finances to unlocking your full potential in personal growth with actionable advice, personal reflections, and interactive tools designed to transform theory into practice. Each chapter is a stepping stone towards becoming the chief architect of your own life.

Our dialogue throughout this book is like a heart-to-heart with an older friend—someone who's been in your shoes and has graduated to a more senior stage of life. It's a style of communication that aims to be engaging and relatable, with a blend of humor and gravity when tackling the topics that matter most.

I invite you to read these pages with an open heart and a keen mind. It's a manual for life, a companion on your road to adulthood.

Let me share a moment from my own life when I stood at a crossroads, overwhelmed by the choices and challenges ahead. I realized that while the pathway to adulthood is universal, the experience is uniquely personal. This book is born from those experiences, aiming to light the way for others.

As we set off on the voyage of this book together, I am thrilled by your willingness to grow, learn, and transform your approach to adult life.

Your decision to read this is a brave first step toward mastering the intricacies of adulthood. You're not alone in your journey; this book is a testament to our shared commitment to your success.

Welcome to *Real-World Life Skills for Young Adults*. Let's turn the page together and begin this transformative adventure!

CHAPTER ONE
CAREER PLANNING AND JOB SEARCH

> *"The best way to predict the future is to create it."*
>
> — PETER DRUCKER

In adulthood, the quest to build and maintain a fulfilling career often takes center stage, not just for obvious reasons related to financial security but also for personal growth, joy, and satisfaction. This chapter presents ways to identify your career passions—passion is a critical element often glossed over in the rush to achieve societal markers of success. A career aligned with your passions supports your job satisfaction and propels you towards excellence in your field, making the work you do not just a job—but a true calling.

1.1 IDENTIFYING YOUR CAREER PASSIONS

Self-Assessment for Career Clarity

This process begins with introspection, looking inward to uncover the layers of your personality, strengths, weaknesses, and—most importantly—the activities that ignite your spirit! This self-assessment is not a quick checklist but a thoughtful exploration of what motivates you, what you value in life, and where your skills lie. Tools like the Myers-Briggs Type Indicator or the StrengthsFinder can offer insights, but equally valuable are moments of reflection on past experiences that brought you joy and fulfillment. It's about recognizing patterns in your field of interest and the challenges that you enjoy—whether creative problem-solving, helping others, or building something tangible.

The Role of Passion in Your Career

The significance of aligning career choices with personal passions cannot be overstated. Daniel H. Pink, in his 2009 book *Drive: The Surprising Truth About What Motivates Us,* emphasizes autonomy, mastery, and purpose as key motivators. Careers aligned with personal passions inherently fulfill these criteria, offering a sense of purpose and the motivation to achieve mastery. The result is heightened job satisfaction (you love your work!), superior performance, and, often, a positive impact on the broader community. Such alignment ensures that an underlying motivation fuels your perseverance, even on challenging days.

Exploring Career Options

With a clearer understanding of your passions, the next step is to explore the vast number of career options available. This exploration is not a straight, linear path but a web of possibilities, each with pros and cons. Consider informational interviews, shadowing professionals in fields of your interest, or even taking on internships or volunteer positions to gain firsthand experience.

These real-world experiences provide invaluable insights into your day-to-day responsibilities and the kind of work environment you might join, helping to refine your understanding of where your passions could best be applied.

Setting Career Goals

Armed with insights into your passions and the relevant potential career paths, it's time to set concrete goals. This planning phase bridges the gap between abstract passions and tangible outcomes. Goals should be set with flexibility, acknowledging the fluid nature of career development. Short-term goals include acquiring specific skills or completing relevant courses, while long-term goals focus on broader career milestones. Regularly revisiting and adjusting these goals ensure they remain aligned with your evolving passions and the dynamic nature of the job market.

Seeking Meaningful Work

In the pursuit of a career that resonates with your passions, the search for meaningful work becomes paramount. Meaningful work is that which contributes to a greater purpose, aligns with your values, and makes a positive impact beyond personal success. This search is deeply personal and varies widely from one individual to another. For some, it might be about innovation and creativity; for others, it might be about social impact or environmental sustainability. The key is to identify what 'meaningful work' looks like for you and seek opportunities that align with this vision.

One of the tools I often use is to ask myself whether the work I am seeking or doing is a plus or minus to society or humanity. What value does it bring to humanity and society?

Throughout this journey of self-discovery and career exploration, remember that the path to finding and pursuing your passions is rarely a straight line.

It's a path marked by questions, reflections, and experiences, each shaping your understanding of your true passions, and how to translate them into a fulfilling and sustainable career.

This chapter serves as your guide through this intricate process, offering strategies, insights, and exercises designed to uncover your unique blend of skills, interests, and values and how they intersect with the real world of work.

1.2 CRAFTING STANDOUT RESUMES AND COVER LETTERS

In our digital age, your resume and cover letter are usually your first interactions with potential employers, acting as ambassadors for your professional narrative. When crafted with intention and strategy, these documents can set you apart in a sea of candidates, paving the way for interviews and job opportunities. Creating these crucial documents demands authenticity and tactical presentation, ensuring they showcase your qualifications and capture the essence of your personal brand and professional aspirations.

Resume Fundamentals

At the heart of every impactful resume lies clarity and conciseness, presenting your achievements and experience in a manner that resonates with the reader (a busy employer). The key components —*contact information, professional summary, work experience, education, and skills*—are woven together to tell the compelling story of your career journey to date. Each element serves a purpose, from highlighting your technical skills to describing your career milestones. Achievement-based statements become the linchpin of this narrative, quantifying your accomplishments in a way that conveys your tangible value to past employers. This method illuminates your capabilities and provides a glimpse into your potential impact in future roles.

The Art of Personal Branding on Paper

Your resume and cover letter are summaries of your professional life that reflect your brand. Infusing these documents with your unique identity as a worker requires introspection into what sets you apart—your values, strengths, and the distinctive blend of experiences you bring to the table. This personal branding exercise transcends the mere listing of job duties, inviting you to articulate your professional identity and how it aligns with the ethos of the companies you aspire to join. Writing a narrative that weaves your individuality into your professional achievements invites prospective employers to see not just a candidate—but a person with a vision and values that resonate with their organizational culture.

Customizing Applications for Each Job

The era of one-size-fits-all resumes and cover letters has long passed. In its place is a nuanced approach to job applications, where customization reigns supreme. Tailoring your resume and cover letter for each application is not merely about changing a few keywords; it's about aligning your document's narrative with the ethos and needs of the company and role you're applying for. This alignment demonstrates your genuine interest in the position and ability to pinpoint and communicate how your skills and experiences address the role's specific challenges.

ATS Optimization

In the labyrinth of modern job searching, Applicant Tracking Systems (ATS) represents both a hurdle and a necessity. ATS allows employers to sift through countless applications to find matches based on predetermined criteria. Optimizing your resume for ATS involves incorporating relevant keywords from the job description while maintaining the natural flow of your professional narrative. This optimization ensures that your resume passes through the ATS filters and retains its readability and impact when it reaches human hands. Strategies such as using standard section headings and avoiding graphics or tables that could confuse the ATS algorithms are crucial in this process.

Overcoming Common Resume Challenges

Resume writing often involves confronting and overcoming a series of challenges, from gaps in employment to career transitions. These perceived hurdles, however, can become opportunities to showcase your resilience, adaptability, and growth. For employment gaps, the focus shifts to how you used that time productively, whether through further education, freelance work, or personal projects that contributed to your professional development. Similarly, career changers have a unique chance to highlight the transferable skills and fresh perspectives they bring to their new field.

By framing such challenges as narratives of growth and learning, your resume and cover letter will offer a richer, more nuanced portrait of your professional journey.

Ultimately, your resume and cover letter serve as the initial threads in the fabric of your professional narrative, weaving together your past achievements with your future aspirations. They cover your career's unique story, inviting potential employers to picture you as a future contributor to their organization's success. Through careful crafting, strategic personal branding, and thoughtful customization, these documents become powerful tools in your job search arsenal, opening doors to opportunities that align with your passions and professional goals.

1.3 MASTERING THE JOB INTERVIEW

Handling job interviews successfully requires a multifaceted approach, blending research, practice, and the nuanced art of communication to create a memorable and positive impression. This segment explores the strategies that underpin adequate interview preparation, from the initial research phase to the nuanced dynamics of post-interview follow-up.

Preparation Is Key

A well-prepared candidate showcases their qualifications and genuine interest in the role and the company. Researching the company's history, culture, and recent achievements provides a solid foundation for understanding. It enables you to tailor your responses to align with the company's mission and values. Similarly, rehearsing responses to common interview questions allows you to refine your delivery, ensuring that your answers are concise and have a good impact. This preparation extends to understanding the job description in detail, enabling you to anticipate questions related to your ability to fulfill the role's requirements and to articulate how your experiences and skills make you the ideal candidate.

The STAR Method

Effectively communicating your past achievements and how they've prepared you for the role you're interviewing for can be achieved through the STAR method. This acronym, which stands for Situation, Task, Action, and Result, is a technique that provides a structured approach to answering behavioral interview questions. By framing your responses to highlight a specific situation, the task at hand, the actions you took, and the results of those actions, you provide a straightforward, concise narrative demonstrating your problem-solving capabilities and impact. The STAR method helps structure your thoughts and ensures that your answers are directly relevant to the question—showcasing your ability to reflect on your experiences and draw important lessons from them.

Body Language and First Impressions

The silent lingo of body language plays a pivotal role in shaping the interviewer's first impression of you. From the moment you enter the room, your posture, handshake, eye contact, and even how you manage nervous habits will convey confidence, enthusiasm, and professionalism. Maintaining an open posture, making consistent but natural eye contact, and offering a firm handshake signal engagement and confidence. Additionally, mirroring the interviewer's body language can create a rapport. Being mindful of these non-verbal cues will enhance the impact of your overall communication during the interview.

Asking Insightful Questions

The questions you ask during an interview are as revealing as your answers, demonstrating your critical thinking skills and engagement with the role and the company. Crafting questions that delve into the specifics of the role, the team's dynamics, or the company's future directions shows a depth of interest and an eagerness to contribute meaningfully. These inquiries should stem from your research and genuine, motivated curiosity about aspects of the job or company not readily found on their website or other public materials. By asking insightful questions, you gather valuable information and reinforce your suitability and enthusiasm for the role.

Post-Interview Strategies

The dialogue does not end when the interview concludes; follow-up actions can significantly influence the outcome. A timely thank-you email reiterates your interest in the position. It provides an opportunity to briefly reinforce why you are the ideal candidate, strengthening any points you wish you had elaborated further upon during the interview. If a significant amount of time passes with no response, a polite inquiry about the status of your application keeps you in the loop and demonstrates your continued interest. For interviews that do not result in a job offer, requesting feedback reflects a commitment to professional growth. Such feedback offers insights into areas for improvement or clarifies how you can better align with potential roles in the future.

You will position yourself as the best candidate and a compelling choice for the role through meticulous preparation, mastery of storytelling techniques, awareness of non-verbal cues, engagement through thoughtful questions, and strategic post-interview follow-up.

1.4 NETWORKING STRATEGIES FOR BUILDING PROFESSIONAL RELATIONSHIPS

Networking fundamentals

Networking, often misconstrued as a series of transactional interactions aimed at immediate personal gain, revolves around cultivating mutually beneficial relationships over time. It encompasses the power of human connection in the professional realm, a catalyst for opportunities that lie beyond the reach of conventional job-searching methods. This intricate web of professional relationships provides a support system, a source of inspiration, and, perhaps most crucially, a bridge to seldom-advertised work opportunities.

Understanding the nuances of effective networking begins with recognizing its dual nature—it is both an art and a science. The science aspect involves strategic planning:

- Identifying key individuals within your desired industry.
- Understanding their influence.
- Determining the best approach to initiate contact.

The art, however, lies in genuine interaction, the ability to engage in meaningful conversations that transcend merely shallow professional courtesies, and the skill to nurture these relationships over time without an overt expectation of reciprocity.

In our era of digital connectivity, platforms like LinkedIn have emerged as valuable tools for professional networking. They offer the unique ability to connect with industry leaders, peers, and potential mentors across the globe. Yet, the effectiveness of these social media platforms hinges on the quality of engagement. The first step is crafting a profile that accurately reflects your professional narrative and aspirations. Beyond that, active participation in discussions, sharing of relevant content, and thoughtful engagement with others' posts serve as the digital equivalent of in-person networking efforts. These actions, driven by your authenticity, lay the groundwork for meaningful connections that can lead to work opportunities.

Effective Networking Strategies

The strategy for effective networking extends to the organization and participation in informational interviews. This practice provides insights into the realities of a role or industry while expanding your professional network. Approaching these interactions with the mindset of curiosity rather than self-promotion, gives them learning opportunities and fosters connections based on mutual interests and professional respect. In these conversations, the most genuine connections are forged, often leading to guidance, mentorship, and, on occasion, direct opportunities.

Building and Maintaining Your Network

Building and maintaining a network demands more than initial outreach and engagement; it requires consistent effort in sharing relevant information and showing genuine interest in the individual's professional journey. Small efforts reinforce the value placed on the relationship, ensuring that your network remains a vibrant ecosystem of professional support.

Networking Etiquette

Adhering to professional networking etiquette is paramount; It includes respecting boundaries, understanding the appropriate contexts for making requests, and expressing gratitude for any assistance or advice offered. Acknowledging that each individual's time is valuable, and their willingness to engage with you is a true gift, will foster a culture of mutual respect. The most enduring professional relationships are nurtured within this respectful framework of genuine engagement.

Through strategic engagement, sustained effort, and adherence to respect and authenticity, networking transcends its utilitarian roots and becomes a cornerstone of lifelong professional growth.

1.5 NAVIGATING JOB OFFERS AND NEGOTIATIONS

Evaluating Job Offers

When the tide of your job search brings you to the shores of a formal job offer, the waves of excitement often coincide with the undercurrents of decision-making complexities! At this juncture, understanding the multifaceted nature of job offers becomes crucial. Beyond the numerical allure of a salary, several elements warrant careful consideration. For instance, benefits, such as health insurance, retirement plans, and paid leave, carry considerable weight in the overall value of an offer. Equally, the intangible aspects, like company culture, growth opportunities, and work-life balance policies, offer insights into how well the position aligns with your personal and professional aspirations. Evaluating these components requires a holistic approach, balancing immediate gains with long-term career development and personal fulfillment.

The Art of Salary Negotiation

The negotiation process, often perceived with trepidation, unfolds as a dialogue grounded in mutual respect and shared goals. Armed with research on industry standards, you enter this dialogue not as a petitioner but as a professional advocating for your worth. This approach pivots on the understanding that negotiation is not about confrontation but about seeking alignment between your professional value and the company's compensation framework. Techniques such as expressing enthusiasm for the role while articulating your case for a higher offer and using evidence of your accomplishments and market rates are keystones of effective negotiation. Maintaining a stance of flexibility signals your willingness to find common ground, laying the foundation for a positive future working relationship.

Declining offers gracefully

There are moments when, despite the allure of an offer, the path forward necessitates declining. This decision, often fraught with anxiety about burning bridges, instead opens avenues for maintaining professional relationships when handled with tact. A decline communicated with sincerity, emphasizing the careful consideration given to the offer and expressing gratitude for the opportunity, reflects professionalism. It's beneficial to articulate, albeit broadly, the reasons behind your decision, offering feedback that can foster goodwill. This transparency and a door-left-open demeanor ensure that the professional bonds forged during the interview remain intact, preserving a potential offer of future opportunities.

Accepting offers

Conversely, accepting an offer that aligns with your career goals and personal values marks the beginning of a brand-new chapter. This step, while celebratory, demands meticulous attention to detail. A thorough review of the offer letter, employment contract, and any associated documents is imperative to ensure clarity on the terms of employment, including the role's responsibilities, reporting lines, and performance evaluation criteria. This scrutiny extends to understanding the specifics of the compensation package—including salary, bonuses, benefits, and any conditional clauses. Questions should be clarified when they arise; you are seeking to eliminate ambiguities rather than challenge terms. This inquiry, rooted in the desire for mutual understanding, sets the stage for a relationship characterized by open communication and mutual respect.

How you convey your decision when accepting an offer reflects your professional ethos. A prompt response, mirroring the formal tone of the offer with a written acceptance, underscores your commitment and enthusiasm for the position. This correspondence, while celebratory in tone, reiterates the critical terms of the offer, ensuring a shared understanding between you and the employer. Additionally, it serves as an opportune moment to express gratitude for the opportunity and to inquire about the next steps, demonstrating your eagerness to contribute to the company's success.

The journey from evaluating job offers through negotiation to either declining or accepting positions reveals itself as a complex interplay of decision-making, strategic communication, and professional integrity. At each juncture, the principles of thorough evaluation, respectful negotiation, tactful decline, and meticulous acceptance will guide your steps, ensuring that each decision—whether to move forward with an opportunity or to step away—is made with a clear understanding of its implications for your career path.

1.6 RESILIENCE IN REJECTION: TURNING NO´S INTO OPPORTUNITIES

Dealing with rejection

Facing rejection is an inevitable aspect of the job search process, yet it can forge the spirit of ambition that fuels one's career aspirations. While initially disheartening, the sting of a declined application serves as a crucible for personal and professional growth when approached with resilience and a forward-looking mindset. This segment sheds light on transforming the shadow of rejection into a catalyst for opportunity, weaving through strategies for coping, learning, and ultimately *thriving* in the face of setbacks.

Understanding your emotional response post-rejection requires an initial acknowledgment of the feelings it stirs—disappointment, self-doubt, and frustration are natural experiences. However, lingering too long in this state risks entrenching a mindset contradictory to growth. Transitioning from this phase involves a deliberate shift towards constructive reflection, viewing each rejection not as a verdict on one's worth but as a single data point in a broader spectrum of opportunities. Herein lies the potential for resilience—a quality that, much like a muscle, strengthens with exercise. Engaging in activities reaffirming one's competence and value—through continuing education, creative pursuits, or contributing to community projects—can reinvigorate the sense of self-worth perhaps eroded by rejection.

Learning from feedback

While often a daunting exercise, obtaining feedback post-rejection is instrumental in honing the approach to future applications. Constructive criticism, when sought with genuine openness, illuminates the gaps between one's current offerings and the expectations of potential employers. This pursuit of insight necessitates a balance between tenacity and tact; not all rejections will be accompanied by detailed feedback, yet a polite and concise request can sometimes open doors to invaluable advice. In synthesizing this feedback, one can identify patterns—perhaps a recurring skill gap or a misalignment in communicated values—that can guide you in refining your skill set and presentation.

Maintaining motivation

Maintaining motivation amidst a succession of rejections demands a reorientation of perspective, focusing on the *process* rather than the *outcome.* Setting small, achievable goals—completing a new certification, enhancing a portfolio piece, or expanding one's network—

embeds the job search within a larger context of personal development. Celebrating these incremental achievements fosters a sense of progress, buffering against the erosion of morale. Moreover, placing oneself within a community of peers, mentors, or accountability partners can provide both a source of encouragement and a sounding board for strategies, reminding you of the universality of rejection and the resilience it can inspire.

Turning rejection into opportunity

The transformation of rejection into opportunity often unfolds unexpectedly, with closed doors redirecting one's path in unforeseen directions. Stories abound of individuals who redirected their focus towards entrepreneurial ventures, further education, or alternative career paths aligned more authentically with their passions and skills—all in the aftermath of job rejections. Others have found that rejection, while initially seeming like a detour, serendipitously prepared them for roles of more excellent alignment, responsibility, or fulfillment that lay just over the horizon. Resilience in the face of rejection can catalyze a journey back to the drawing-board and into realms of previously unimagined possibility.

In this light, rejection assumes a new guise—not as an endpoint but as a juncture, a moment of pause that invites reflection, learning, and redirection. It challenges you to distill clarity from disappointment, refine goals with fresh insights, and persist with a resilience fortified by experience. This reframing of rejection as an integral (albeit challenging) component of your job search equips you with the tenacity to continue, the agility to pivot, the wisdom to learn, and the courage to explore new avenues!

1.7 THE GIG ECONOMY: OPPORTUNITIES AND CHALLENGES

Understanding the gig economy

In the 21st-century job market, where traditional career pathways blur into a mosaic of project-based and freelance endeavors, the gig economy emerges as both a playground and a battleground for modern professionals. Propelled by technological advancements and changing work-life preferences, this shift is redefining notions of employment, offering a range of opportunities with unique challenges.

The "gig economy" describes a labor market characterized by the prevalence of short-term contracts or freelance work as opposed to permanent jobs. Its rise signals a significant transformation in the job market, driven by individuals' desire for flexibility, autonomy, and the opportunity to tailor work to their personal and professional ambitions. Platforms like Upwork, Freelancer, and Fiverr are conduits connecting skilled professionals with businesses and individuals needing their services. These digital marketplaces democratize access to opportunities, allowing talents to showcase their skills to a global audience.

Finding gig work

Finding gig work that aligns with one's skills and career goals requires a strategic approach. It begins with your profile—clearly articulating one's value proposition, a concise statement highlighting unique skills, experiences, and the specific benefits one brings to potential clients. This clarity serves as a beacon, guiding the search for opportunities that match one's skill set and resonate with personal interests and professional aspirations. Crafting a compelling profile on gig platforms, complemented by a portfolio showcasing previous work, is a magnet for potential employers. Online and offline networking further amplifies visibility, opening doors to opportunities that might not be advertised on traditional job boards.

Managing gig work

Managing multiple gigs demands a refined approach to time management and financial planning, skills that ensure the successful completion of projects and the sustainability of one's freelance career. Effective time management hinges on prioritizing tasks, setting realistic deadlines, and, most crucially, setting boundaries to prevent burnout. Tools such as Trello or Asana can aid in organizing projects and tracking progress, while dedicated work hours help maintain a healthy work-life balance. On the other hand, financial planning involves:

- A meticulous approach to budgeting.
- Accounting for irregular income streams.
- Setting aside funds for taxes, savings, and retirement.

This financial discipline ensures resilience in the face of the gig economy's inherent unpredictability.

Long-term considerations

The long-term implications of gig work on career development and financial stability invite careful consideration. On one hand, the gig economy offers a platform for continuous learning, allowing individuals to diversify their skills and experience across industries and projects. This exposure can accelerate career growth, fostering a diverse portfolio and a professional network spanning multiple sectors. On the other hand, the absence of traditional employment benefits such as health insurance, retirement plans, and job security poses significant risks. Navigating this landscape requires a proactive stance on personal development and financial security, including investing in skill advancement, seeking out professional communities for support, and exploring financial products designed for the self-employed.

In this context, the gig economy presents a duality that encapsulates the freedom and fulfillment of pursuing work that aligns with one's passions against economic uncertainty and the absence of conventional career growth markers. It underscores the evolving nature of work, where adaptability, continuous learning, and financial acumen become vital pillars supporting the pursuit of professional autonomy. Within this framework, success is not merely measured by monetary gain but by the ability to navigate the complexities of freelance work, giving opportunities for growth while mitigating the risks associated with this mode of employment.

Chapter 1 Action Summary:

1. Get a free self-assessment test from https://www.16personalities.com/
2. Explore career options that match your personality and passion test result. https://www.careerexplorer.com/
3. Look back on all your past experiences and moments that brought you joy and fulfillment, and relate those moments with what you were doing—that could help you identify your passion.
4. Volunteer to shadow a professor's research, volunteer work, and apply for an internship in your field of interest to validate your interest.
5. Craft your personal resume and cover letter. Refer to Google Doc resume templates: Open a new Google Doc in your Google Drive, click on Template Gallery at the top right, and look for resumes.
6. Refer to References [3,4] at the end of this book for more resume template samples and tips on personal branding, customization, and optimization.
7. Research from media sites (YouTube, LinkedIn) for common interview questions related to your field of interest
8. Apply STAR method (Situation, Task, Action, Result) to draft up your answers for behavior interview questions.
9. Search media sites or ChatGPT to prepare Insightful questions that you need to ask at the interview related to the job or company that you are interested in or want to have an interview with
10. Prepare a Post-Interview thank you email. ChatGPT will definitely help you draft up one in minutes.
11. Refer to Reference [5] for additional tips and resources
12. Research on the LinkedIn platform in your field of interest. Identify key individuals who show credibility, influence, and knowledge in your field of interest. Follow their posts, add comments, questions, and compliments to show your genuine impression, and admire their works. Request permission to

connect and network with them to learn and build relationships.

13. Refer to Reference [6] for additional tips and resources
14. Review and understand the key items in a job offer package.
15. Research the new job offer salary range in the industry of your interest.
16. Refer to Reference [7] for additional tips and resources
17. Prepare an email reply to job application rejections politely asking for feedback for improvement and prepare better for future job applications. ChatGPT can help you draft one quickly.
18. Review your self-assessment test result and see if your values, passions, and strengths are also aligned with other alternative careers.
19. Look into gig work platforms such as Upwork, Freelancer, and Fiverr to find freelance work that matches your skills and strengths that you can sign up for contract work.
20. Looking into online course platforms such as Udemy.com and Coursera.com and enrolling in courses of interest for gig work or enhancing job skills.
21. Refer to Reference [8] for additional tips and resources

CHAPTER TWO
SELF-DISCIPLINE AND TIME MANAGEMENT

> *"Discipline is the bridge between goals and accomplishment."*
>
> — JIM ROHN

2.1 SELF-DISCIPLINE:

Self-discipline is essential for personal development as it enables individuals to maintain focus, consistency, and motivation. It provides the foundation for achieving long-term goals by helping individuals overcome short-term temptations and emotional impulses. With self-discipline, we can effectively manage our time, prioritize tasks, and consistently work toward our aspirations.

The benefits of self-discipline include enhanced productivity, better physical health, and improved mental well-being. It allows individuals to stick to healthy habits, leading to greater accomplishments and a sense of satisfaction. Self-discipline also contributes to financial stability, stronger relationships, and a balanced life.

Effective techniques for forging self-discipline include:

- Setting clear, specific, and achievable goals.
- Breaking larger goals into smaller, manageable tasks.
- Developing good habits through repetition and routine.
- Practicing mindfulness and self-awareness.
- Seeking support from mentors, coaches, or accountability partners.

2.2 PRIORITIZING DAILY TASKS: THE EISENHOWER MATRIX CONCEPT

Prioritizing tasks emerges as an important tool of control in our busy lives. It's not merely about ticking off items on a to-do list but understanding the weight or significance of each task and its impact on our personal and professional landscape. This chapter delves into the Eisenhower Box, a tool for organization and strategic discernment, offering insight into how we can sift through all the noise to focus on what genuinely *matters.*

The Eisenhower Decision Matrix, known as the Eisenhower Box, is like a ship´s compass in the tumultuous sea of obligations—guiding users to categorize tasks based on urgency and importance. Its beauty lies in its simplicity: a quadrant that separates tasks into four categories:

- Urgent and Important,
- Important but not Urgent,
- Urgent but not Important,
- Neither Urgent nor Important.

This framework isn't just about organization; it's about making strategic decisions that align with our deepest values *and* long-term objectives.

Imagine standing in a kitchen on a Sunday evening, the week's groceries sprawled across the counter, and a calendar full of commitments and aspirations in the week ahead. Here, the Eisenhower Box transforms things from concept to practice. Urgent and important tasks, like setting aside time preparing meals for the week to maintain a healthy diet, take precedence. In contrast, albeit seeming urgent in the "ping" of notifications, scrolling through social media falls into the quadrant of neither urgent nor important, a distraction from more meaningful pursuits. This real-life application extends beyond the kitchen, touching every aspect of life where time is the currency, and how we spend it dictates the rich experience of our days.

Balancing Urgent vs. Important Tasks

The crux of mastering the Eisenhower Box lies in the distinction between urgency and importance—a task's loudness doesn't necessarily denote its significance. Urgent tasks often masquerade as critical, their immediacy demanding attention, yet, upon reflection, their contribution to our overarching goals may be quite minimal. Conversely, important tasks that propel us toward our aspirations frequently whisper for attention, and are easy to overlook in the clamor. Cultivating the discipline to pause and *evaluate* tasks through the Eisenhower lens ensures that our efforts are not just reactive, but aligned with our purpose.

Avoiding Common Pitfalls

A trap many of us fall into is the conflation of urgency with importance, a misstep that can divert energy and resources from tasks that will genuinely advance our goals. Another pitfall lies in neglecting the important but not urgent quadrant—the home of strategic planning, personal development, and relationships. While not screaming for immediate attention, these tasks are the building blocks of a fulfilled and balanced life. Recognizing and avoiding these common missteps, guided by the Eisenhower Box, shifts the paradigm from being busy, to being effective—a distinction that marks the difference between motion and progress.

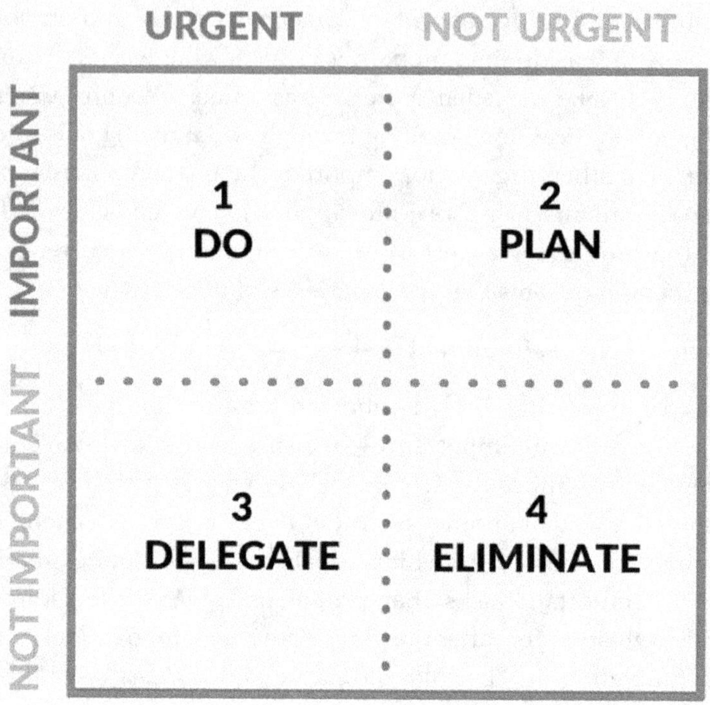

Reference[44-45]

The Eisenhower Box stands not merely as a time management method but as a philosophy of life management, where the discernment of urgency versus importance guides daily decisions. In adopting this framework, we take up the power to navigate through life's demands with purpose and intention, ensuring that our time—our most precious resource—is invested in pursuits that *truly matter*.

2.3 DIGITAL TOOLS FOR TIME MANAGEMENT

In this 21st-century era, where the digital realm is woven through the fabric of our daily endeavors, the choice of digital tools for time management transcends mere preference—it morphs into a strategic decision that underpins our productivity. This critical selection process needs your discerning eye to sift through the myriad options to pinpoint tools that resonate with your unique rhythm of productivity and time management challenges. It is not about adopting tools with the most features, but about embracing those that align seamlessly with your workflow, enhancing efficiency without adding layers of complexity. Identifying these tools involves carefully assessing your daily tasks, refining areas where time could be optimized, and pinpointing the gaps technology could bridge. This reflective analysis paves the way for a tailored approach, ensuring that the chosen digital tools serve as catalysts for productivity, rather than distractions.

One of my go-to digital apps for prioritizing my tasks is the "Focus Matrix" app, which can be downloaded and used to apply the Eisenhower Box technique very effectively.

Reference[46-48] for additional tools

Among the plethora of options in time management apps, certain ones distinguish themselves through their functionality and ability to integrate into the user's life with minimal friction. For instance, apps specializing in the Pomodoro Technique offer a structured framework that breaks work into intervals, promoting focus and rest in a rhythm that enhances mental agility. Others, designed for project management, function as digital nerve centers, where tasks, deadlines, and collaborations converge, offering a bird's eye view of progress and pending tasks. Then, habit-tracking apps and digital mirrors reflect our daily practices, nudging us towards consistency and growth. Each of these tools, distinct in its purpose, shares a common aim—to find islands of productivity in the ocean of daily tasks, enabling users to navigate their responsibilities with precision and grace.

Integrating these digital aids into our daily routines is challenging, requiring a deliberate approach that melds technology with our human element. It involves creating habits around the usage of the tools, embedding them into the start and end of each day as bookends that frame our productivity narrative. Strategies for seamless integration include setting specific times for reviewing tasks and progress, thereby creating a rhythm that ensures these tools are actively engaged. It also involves leveraging the synchronicity between devices, ensuring that irrespective of the medium—be it smartphone, tablet, or desktop—you remain tethered to your tasks and goals, a continuity that reinforces commitment and focus.

Yet, as technology evolves at a breakneck pace, the onus falls on us to keep abreast of the tools that could enhance our productivity. Staying updated with new technologies and tools is an active pursuit that requires our curiosity and proactive stance. It involves regular exploration of emerging apps, participation in forums and discussions that shed light on the uses of innovative technology, and an openness to experimentation. Doing this, while time-consuming, offers the reward of discovery, unearthing tools that could redefine the contours of your productivity, propelling you towards your goals with renewed vigor. Moreover, it supports a commitment to continuous improvement, recognizing that the productivity landscape is ever-evolving, and our strategies must evolve too.

2.4 OVERCOMING PROCRASTINATION

Understanding the Root Causes

Procrastination—where tasks loom large and intentions are shackled, has psychological roots, and understanding this offers liberation. Procrastination stems from a mix of fear, perfectionism, and a skewed perception of time. Fear of failure paralyzes action, perfectionism sets unattainable standards leading to delays, and misjudging task duration breeds false confidence in future productivity.

Addressing these issues starts with acknowledgment. Recognizing fear as a natural response allows you to reevaluate outcomes and reduce anxiety. Combatting perfectionism involves you setting realistic standards, valuing progress over perfection. Correcting time perception requires you to accurately estimate task durations and create a realistic schedule that balances work—and rest.

Strategies to Beat Procrastination

Strategies to overcome procrastination focus on transforming intention into action. Breaking tasks into smaller steps makes them more approachable, and establishing deadlines creates structure. A well-organized workspace reduces distractions and enhances focus. Setting meaningful goals and celebrating small wins builds a cycle of positive reinforcement. Visualization techniques and establishing routines ease transitions into productive states, while accountability will add external motivation.

Overcoming procrastination involves recognizing its root causes, confronting them, and then applying practical strategies *to turn intentions into actions*. This journey, marked by self-awareness and adaptability, leads to a more focused, productive life.

Reference[49] for additional resources.

2.5 SETTING AND ACHIEVING PERSONAL GOALS

This process of setting and achieving personal goals, while intricate in its design, demands not just the articulation of your desires, but a systematic approach that transforms the vision into the tangible—the dream into the achievable. Within this alchemy of ambition, the true art of goal-setting is revealed, demanding both imagination and pragmatism in equal measure.

Goal-Setting Techniques

This transformative process begins with exploring goal-setting techniques. Among these techniques, visualization is a practice that breathes life into goals, rendering them in vivid detail in the mind's eye. This vibrant and compelling mental imagery serves as inspiration and a compass, orienting our actions toward realizing these envisioned futures. Coupled with this is the technique of writing down goals, a simple act that lends weight to intentions, transforming them from fleeting thoughts into commitments inscribed solidly in the physical world. This practice, supported by studies indicating a higher likelihood of achievement of *written* goals, underscores the power of manifesting our aspirations in tangible forms.

Breaking Down Goals

The challenge, of course, lies not in setting goals but in their realization. Here, the task of breaking down larger goals into manageable, actionable steps becomes critical. This segmentation ensures that each step is clear, achievable, and directed toward the ultimate objective. By dissecting ambitious goals down into smaller components, the path forward becomes less daunting, each step a manageable stride rather than a leap into the void! This approach clarifies the immediate actions required and builds useful momentum, as completing each step fuels the motivation to then proceed to the next.

Integral to this methodology is the SMART goal framework, (remember we applied it to the financial savings plan earlier in the book). To highlight it again, SMART is an acronym that describes the goal-setting process along with criteria designed to enhance the likelihood of success.

SMART Goals are crafted to be:

- **S**pecific: Offering clarity and direction
- **M**easurable: Providing tangible benchmarks for progress
- **A**chievable: Ensuring that goals are within reach
- **R**elevant: Aligning with broader life ambitions
- **T**ime-bound: Anchored within a defined timeframe.

Reference[51] for additional resources.

This framework serves as a litmus test for the viability of goals, ensuring that they possess the qualities necessary for realization. It imbues the goal-setting process with a structured rigor, changing the *aspirational* into the *operational.*

Tracking Progress

Progress tracking becomes a critical element in this process. This monitoring, meticulous in its execution, involves regular reviews of achievements against set benchmarks, a practice that offers a measure of advancement and a good source of motivation. It allows for the adjustment of strategies in response to unforeseen obstacles or changes in circumstances, ensuring that your approach remains dynamic and responsive. Moreover, this tracking fosters a sense of accountability, a commitment to the ongoing journey of goal-achievement.

Celebrating Milestones

Within this journey, celebrating milestones serves as a vital source of encouragement and renewal of purpose. These celebrations, markers of progress along the path, offer pause for reflection, appreciation, and reinvigoration. They remind us that the pursuit of goals, though often challenging, is punctuated with moments of achievement that deserve recognition.

As we close this exploration of goal-setting and achievement, we are reminded of the broader narrative encompassing our efforts—the ongoing quest for fulfillment and the realization of our potential. This journey, marked by the milestones of our achievements and the lessons gleaned along the way, prepares us for all the challenges and opportunities of adulthood.

Chapter 2 Action Summary:

1. Apply the Eisenhower Matrix technique to prioritize your daily tasks.
2. Download the Focus Matrix app to your phone and apply it to your daily tasks.
3. Apply the SMART goals method to all your goal-setting. Break down big or long-term tasks into small chunks that are easier to achieve within a time-bound target, and celebrate along the way.

CHAPTER THREE
YOUR MONEY MINDSET, BUDGET AND SAVING GOALS

> *"A penny saved is a penny earned."*
>
> — BENJAMIN FRANKLIN

In a world where life's soundtrack is often composed of digital beeps signaling completed transactions, and notifications of financial ebbs and flows, understanding your relationship with money is very much like learning a new language—a language that, once mastered, can transform your reality. This mastery begins not with numbers on a ledger but with cultivating a mindset attuned to abundance and growth. Financial well-being, after all, extends far beyond the balance in your bank account; it's deeply rooted in the psychological soil from which your attitudes and behaviors around money emerge and flourish.

3.1 CRAFTING YOUR FINANCIAL IDENTITY: DISCOVERING YOUR MONEY MINDSET

Mindset Shifts

Transitioning from a scarcity mindset to one of abundance is like changing the lens through which you view the world. A scarcity mindset, focusing on limitation and fear of loss, narrows your vision, obscuring opportunities for growth and prosperity. In contrast, an abundance mindset expands your horizon, fostering an openness to possibilities. It's the difference between seeing a fixed pie and recognizing that it can grow. This shift doesn't happen overnight but evolves through conscious practice and reflection. It involves challenging ingrained beliefs about money, often passed down through family, and replacing them with affirmations reinforcing a sense of abundance and possibility.

Personal Values and Money

Aligning your financial goals with your core values creates a compass that guides your monetary decisions, ensuring they resonate with your broader life aspirations. This alignment is crucial for sustaining motivation and fulfillment in your financial journey. For instance, if freedom and travel are core values, shaping your financial goals to save for adventures aligns your money management with your passions. This congruence between values and financial objectives infuses your life with meaning, transforming saving money from being a chore into a joyful pursuit of your passions.

Visualization and Goal-Setting

Visualizing financial success is a torch illuminating the path to your financial goals. It's about seeing the future you wish to create—a technique athletes and successful entrepreneurs use. For example, when visualizing purchasing your first home, imagine yourself turning the key in the door, stepping inside, and feeling a sense of accomplishment and security. This vivid imagery, rooted in the tangible aspects of your goal, strengthens your emotional and psychological commitment to achieving it. Pairing visualization with specific, actionable goal-setting transforms these mental images into your reality, laying down step-by-step milestones that guide your progress.

Building a Positive Money Mindset

Developing a positive outlook towards managing money is fundamentally about empowerment. It's recognizing that you have control over your financial destiny and that each decision contributes to this narrative—no matter how small. A practice to cultivate such a mindset is to reflect on financial victories regularly, be they as minor as resisting an impulsive purchase, or as significant as reaching a savings milestone. Celebrating these successes reinforces a sense of agency, gradually building a financial identity grounded in positivity and empowerment.

Action checklist:

Take an Interactive Quiz to assess your money mindset with the websites below:

- https://financialfit.com/pages/money-mindset-quiz
- https://lewis-moneymindset.scoreapp.com/?refid2=facebook#:~

These short, engaging quizzes will reveal your underlying attitudes towards money. It will provide insights into areas of strength and opportunities for growth. Based on your answers, you'll receive tailored advice on nurturing an abundance mindset and aligning your financial practices with your core values.

Research like this will prompt deep reflection on personal values and how they intersect with financial goals. This section encourages writing down core values, current financial goals, and how they align or diverge, offering a structured approach to reevaluating and realigning financial objectives with personal aspirations.

The journey to financial well-being is multifaceted, rooted in the practicalities of budgeting and saving and the psychological biases of your relationship with money. By shifting your mindset towards abundance, aligning your financial goals with your core values, embracing the power of visualization, and fostering a positive financial identity, you lay the foundation for a life characterized not by financial stress—but by prosperity and fulfillment. This chapter serves as your guide, offering strategies and practices to cultivate a *healthy* financial mindset, ensuring that your financial decisions propel you towards a future that is prosperous and full of possibility.

3.2 BREAKING FREE FROM FINANCIAL MYTHS: WHAT YOU DIDN'T LEARN IN SCHOOL

Debunking myths

Financial independence stands as a coveted milestone in life, a beacon that many young adults strive toward with zeal. However, the path is often obscured by a dense fog of myths and misconceptions, remnants of a bygone era, and well-intentioned advice that has not weathered the test of time. These myths can lead the unwary astray, far from the shores of financial security and prosperity. It is imperative to chart a course that acknowledges and actively dispels these myths, replacing folklore with 21st century fact, and superstition with strategy.

Educational gaps

Unfortunately, the bedrock of financial literacy finds scant footing in conventional education, leaving a chasm between academic achievement and real-world financial acumen. This profound and pervasive gap underscores the necessity for self-directed learning, a quest for knowledge that moves beyond the confines of textbooks and classrooms. The onus falls upon the individual to seek out resources (like this very book!), mentors, and experiences that illuminate the principles of sound financial management. Pursuing financial literacy becomes not just an act of personal responsibility but a rite of passage into a well-informed adulthood.

Building financial literacy

Building this financial knowledge base outside the traditional educational setting demands a proactive approach and a willingness to delve into topics that range from the rudimentary to the complex. This endeavor is supported by abundant resources—books penned by financial experts, online courses that offer interactive learning experiences, and podcasts that distill wisdom into digestible segments. Each avenue offers unique insights, from the psychological underpinnings of spending habits to the intricacies of investment portfolios. The diversity of perspectives and methodologies enriches the learning journey, equipping you with a versatile toolkit for managing your personal financial life.

Critical thinking

Critical thinking is an important skill in this quest, serving as a shield and compass. It empowers you to scrutinize advice—whether from a financial guru or from a viral social media post—with a discerning eye, separating the grain from the chaff. This analytical approach extends to evaluating financial products and services, encouraging a comparison of fees, benefits, and long-term implications. In cultivating this skill, you learn not only to question, but also to seek evidence, to challenge assumptions, and, in doing so, to forge a path that aligns with your values and specific circumstances.

The myths that pervade the realm of personal finance often masquerade as axioms; their veracity rarely questioned. One such myth posits that credit cards are inherently detrimental to financial health—a tool that inevitably leads to debt and despair. While rooted in legitimate concerns over debt accumulation, this narrative overlooks the positive role that credit cards play in building credit history and facilitating cash flow management. When used judiciously, with balances paid in full each cycle, credit cards emerge not as villains, but as valuable instruments in the financial arsenal.

Another pervasive myth suggests that investing is the exclusive domain of the wealthy—a complex and risky endeavor beyond the reach of the average individual. This misconception stifles financial growth, relegating savings to low-yield accounts that fail to keep up with inflation. Demystifying the practice of investment reveals a spectrum of opportunities accessible to investors of *all* levels, from low-cost index funds that mirror the market's movements, to robo-advisors that automate investment strategies. The key lies in education and gradual engagement, starting with modest investments and escalating as confidence and knowledge grow.

The myth of the self-made financial savant, who navigates the markets with innate and special prowess, casts a long shadow and fosters a sense of inadequacy among those less well-versed in financial matters. This myth neglects the communal nature of financial knowledge, the insights gleaned from shared experiences, successes, and failures. Financial literacy is not a solitary pursuit but a collective journey enriched by the wisdom of the community. Engaging in discussions, whether through online forums, investment clubs, or informal gatherings, dismantles the myth of the lone financier, emphasizing financial learning as a communal endeavor.

In dispelling these myths, you reclaim power over your financial narrative, recognizing that independence is not born of *inherent genius* but of *acquired knowledge* and *deliberate practice*. This empowerment is fortified by recognizing financial education as a lifelong pursuit, an ever-evolving process that adapts to changing circumstances, goals, and economic landscapes. The myths that once obscured the path give way to clarity, illuminating a journey marked not by fear and misconception—but by informed decisions and strategic planning.

3.3 THE POWER OF FINANCIAL GOALS: SETTING AND ACHIEVING YOUR MILESTONES

In personal finance, setting goals is like plotting a course on a map; it defines the destination, and the path to reach it. However, unlike a linear journey from point A to point B, navigating financial aspirations requires a broad as well as detailed understanding of the territory, including the valleys of immediate needs and the peaks of future dreams. This understanding forms the bedrock upon which realistic and motivating financial goals are established, serving not as distant plans but as accessible milestones, each marking progress towards the broader horizon of financial well-being.

Goal-Setting Strategies

This process demands more than mere wishful thinking; it necessitates a systematic approach to translating abstract desires into actionable objectives. It begins with specificity, delineating what might start as vague aspirations into precise targets. For instance, rather than aspiring to, "save more money," a goal is reframed in measurable terms, such as, "save $5,000 for an emergency fund within 12 months." This specificity is complemented by relevance, ensuring each goal aligns with current circumstances and future aspirations, thereby embedding personal significance into every financial milestone. The infusion of timelines further transforms aspirations into real commitments, imposing structure and urgency that galvanize action. This triad of specificity, relevance, and timeliness cultivates fertile ground from which realistic and motivating goals will sprout, each meticulously crafted to propel you *forward* on your financial voyage.

Short-term vs Long-term Financial Goals

The dichotomy between short-term and long-term goals mirrors the sometimes fairly delicate balance between present needs and future aspirations. Short-term goals, often defined as objectives achievable within a year, focus on immediate priorities such as establishing an emergency fund, or paying off credit card debt. These goals serve as stepping stones, providing relatively quick wins that bolster confidence and foster a habit of financial discipline. Conversely, long-term goals, with horizons extending beyond a year, encompass aspirations like retirement savings or home ownership. These goals require persistence and patience, often necessitating sacrifices in the here and now to secure the future vision. Balancing these two goal types prevents the derailment of immediate financial health for future gains, or vice versa, ensuring a holistic approach to financial planning that nurtures both current well-being *and* future prosperity.

Measuring Progress

Tracking your progress toward financial goals transcends mere number-crunching; it is an exercise in reflection and recalibration. Tools such as budgeting apps or spreadsheets offer a digital canvas upon which your financial journey is painted, each entry a brushstroke that brings the picture of financial health into sharper focus. These tools facilitate regular reviews of income, expenditures, and savings, juxtaposing them against set benchmarks to gauge progress. Yet, beyond the obvious quantitative progress, measuring progress also involves qualitative reflection on the strategies employed, the obstacles encountered, and the lessons gleaned. This holistic assessment, conducted regularly, illuminates the path and the terrain ahead, informing adjustments and fine-tuning strategies to move within the ever-evolving financial landscape.

Adjusting Goals

Flexibility in facing life's vicissitudes is paramount; the financial roadmap is not immune to the winds of change. Economic fluctuations, career transitions, and personal milestones such as marriage or the birth of a child necessitate a reassessment of financial goals and the strategies employed to achieve them. This adjustment is not an admission of defeat but an acknowledgment of life's unpredictability. It perhaps involves reevaluating priorities, reallocating resources, and redefining what financial success means in the context of new circumstances. Such adjustments ensure that financial planning remains dynamic—responsive to life's ebbs and flows, and reflects personal growth and changing aspirations.

In the world of personal finance, setting, adjusting and achieving financial goals is both an art and a science. It requires the rigor of strategic planning and the flexibility to adapt to life's changing circumstances. This balance you strike between aspiration and pragmatism, between the immediate and the distant, forms the essence of effective financial planning. It is a process that demands continuous engagement, a commitment to reflection and adjustment, and an unwavering focus on the personal values and aspirations that guide your financial voyage. Through careful goal-setting, balanced prioritization, diligent tracking, and adaptive recalibration, the time spent achieving financial milestones evolves into a rewarding expedition marked by growth, learning, and an ever-expanding horizon of possibilities.

3.4 CREATING YOUR FIRST BUDGET

Understanding Budgeting Principles

Understanding the foundational principles of budgeting is like charting a map for a treasure hunt, where the treasure is not necessarily gold but financial stability and peace of mind. The distinction between *wants* and *needs* forms the compass for this part of the journey. Wants are those tempting sirens that sing to us with the promise of immediate gratification. Needs are the steadfast crew ensuring the ship remains afloat, guiding us through tumultuous seas. Recognizing this difference is important; it allows for allocating resources to ensure survival and well-being—prioritizing shelter, sustenance, and security over the fleeting allure of luxuries.

Creating a Budgeting Mindset

Cultivating a good budgeting mindset shifts the perception of budgeting from a rather draconian measure that shackles one's lifestyle to a liberating tool that empowers financial freedom. The ethos of "pay yourself first" underpins this perspective, advocating allocating resources towards savings and investments before any other expenses. This principle is further refined by the 10-10-10-70 rule:

- 10% for savings in passive investments (eg. S&P 500 index, employer saving funds 401K, HSA)
- 10% for active investings (Stock, bond, Real Estate)
- 10% debt repayment or charities
- 70% dedicated to monthly expenses and lifestyle

This strategy fosters a habit of saving and investing and also ingrains a sense of responsibility and charity, contributing to a well-rounded financial identity.

Other alternative methods, such as the 20-50-30 rule:

- 20% for saving and investing
- 50% for needs or fixed monthly expenses
- 30% for wants and lifestyle costs

Simple Steps to Your First Budget

Creating your first budget starts with a simple yet profound step: listing all sources of income. This enumeration should encompass the primary sources, such as salaries or wages, and any ancillary income, like freelance work, dividends, or occasional bonuses. Following this, the process demands a meticulous listing of monthly expenditures, categorized into essentials—those needs that ensure survival and well-being—and non-essentials, the wants that enhance life's enjoyment.

Though seemingly rudimentary, this exercise lays bare the financial flows, allowing for a clear-eyed assessment of where the money comes from, and where it flows to.

This assessment paves the way for the allocation of expenses, guided by prioritizing needs over wants. It involves a deliberate decision-making process, weighing the significance of each expense against the overarching financial goals. This phase might reveal uncomfortable truths, such as expenditures on wants that actually far exceed what is sustainable, necessitating a recalibration of spending habits. It's a moment of reckoning where choices align with financial realities and aspirations, setting the stage for a balanced budget that accommodates today's necessities *and* tomorrow's dreams.

Adapting Your Budget Over Time

Adapting your budget over time recognizes the dynamic nature of life, where financial circumstances are as subject to change as the seasons. An increase in income, whether through a raise, a new job, or side hustles, offers an opportunity to accelerate toward financial goals, allowing for an increase in savings and investments or even a recalibration of spending toward long-neglected wants. Conversely, a downturn in financial fortune demands a contraction of expenditures and a tightening of the belt, where wants are temporarily sacrificed on the altar of necessity. This adaptability ensures that the budget remains a relevant and valuable tool, a "living document" that evolves with life's ever-changing circumstances.

In this evolution, periodic reviews become opportunities to reflect on the budget's performance against financial goals and life changes. These reviews, conducted with a blend of objectivity and introspection, serve as checkpoints, moments to celebrate achievements or to course-correct in the face of deviations. They demand honesty, a willingness to confront hard truths about spending habits and financial choices, and the courage to implement necessary changes.

Through this continuous process of review and adaptation, the budget matures, moving from being a rudimentary plan into a sophisticated strategy that guides your financial journey.

Thus, the creation and management of a budget unfold not as a static tool but as a dynamic process that mirrors life's complexities. It begins with the foundational principles of distinguishing between wants and needs, evolves through the cultivation of a budgeting mindset that views financial planning as a tool for empowerment, and matures into a sensitive strategy that adapts to life's inevitable changes. Through this process, budgeting sheds its reputation of being an unwelcome constraint, revealing itself as a channel to financial freedom and well-being.

3.5 THE ART OF TRACKING EXPENSES

The Importance of Tracking

The careful observation of where each penny goes when it leaves your wallet or purse is not a tedious chore, but a strategic maneuver in the grand chess game of personal finance! This vigilance against the unseen trickle of funds slipping through seemingly benign daily transactions forms the cornerstone of a budget that doesn't merely exist but *thrives,* underpinning your aspirations for a future built on financial stability. Here, in the granular analysis of expenditures, patterns emerge from the mist, revealing the contours of your financial habits—some aligning with your goals, others veering off course and necessitating recalibration.

Methods of Expense Tracking

When navigating the plethora of methods to track this financial flow, one encounters a spectrum ranging from the tangibility of pen and paper to the sleek precision of digital applications. With its ruled lines and columns, the traditional ledger offers a tangible connection to your financial transactions, each entry a deliberate act of acknowledgment and consideration. Although archaic in the face of technology, this method provides a visceral understanding of spending rhythms, giving you a mindfulness that the clicks of a digital tool may sometimes dilute.

Conversely, the digital realm offers tools that amalgamate efficiency with analytical depth, applications designed not just to record, but to analyze and interpret. These platforms transform raw data into insightful graphs and charts, illuminating trends in spending that might otherwise remain obscured. The choice between these methods hinges on personal preference, the complexity of your financial landscape, and the depth of insight you seek. For some, the simplicity of pen and paper suffices—a mirror to their straightforward financial dealings. For others, the multifaceted analysis offered by digital tools aligns better with their intricate financial setup, offering a record and a roadmap.

Identifying Spending Habits

The act of tracking, irrespective of the medium, serves as a beacon, illuminating the intricacies of your spending habits. Through this lens, behaviors come into focus, patterns revealing themselves with clarity. Impulsive purchases, recurrent yet unnoticed subscriptions, or the slow leak of dining-out expenses form a picture—each contributing to a narrative that might divert resources from more pressing goals. This revelation is not an indictment but an invitation, a prompt for introspection and adjustment, where the efficacy of your financial strategy is continually honed.

Setting Limits and Alerts

With this knowledge, setting limits and alerts becomes tactical play, a preemptive strike against the encroachment of *unplanned* spending. Budgeting applications excel in this domain, offering features that allow you to configure notifications when spending nears predefined limits, a digital guardian against any erosion of your financial resolve. This real-time feedback loop, a dialogue between intention and action, fosters a dynamic approach to budget management, where adjustments are not reactive—but proactive, embedded in the fabric of your financial planning.

Selecting an appropriate budgeting tool is not a decision made lightly but a strategic choice that works with your financial narrative. Choosing comes from discernment in a sea of applications, each boasting many features. It involves critically evaluating each platform's offers against your unique financial situation and goals. Considerations extend beyond the mere functionality of expense tracking to encompass the security of your data, the ability to customize categories, and the integration with your banking and investment accounts. Some may find value in applications that offer a holistic view, integrating expense tracking with investment monitoring and savings goals. Others prioritize simplicity and ease of use—a manageable tool that facilitates a clearer understanding of their financial flow.

In this quest, reviews and recommendations are valuable guides, offering insights into user experiences and the efficacy of the application in real-world scenarios. Yet, beyond the opinions of others lies the ultimate test—personal trial. Many applications offer trial periods and a sandbox to explore their capabilities and gauge their alignment with your financial management style. This hands-on approach ensures that the chosen tool not only meets your current needs but possesses the flexibility to grow with you.

Thus, the art of tracking expenses transcends the mechanical act of recording transactions; it is a practice imbued with strategy and intention. It demands a choice of tools that resonate with your financial ethos, a commitment to regular engagement, and a willingness to adapt, based on the insights gleaned. Though requiring time and effort, this discipline pays dividends in clarity and control, guiding your steps toward a future where financial goals are envisioned and realized.

References [14,15] at the end of this book provide links to more budget tracker apps and articles.

Below are sample Monthly & Annual budget templates available from Google Sheet [1]

(Open a new Google Sheet, click Template gallery on top right - search for Monthly or Annually budget)

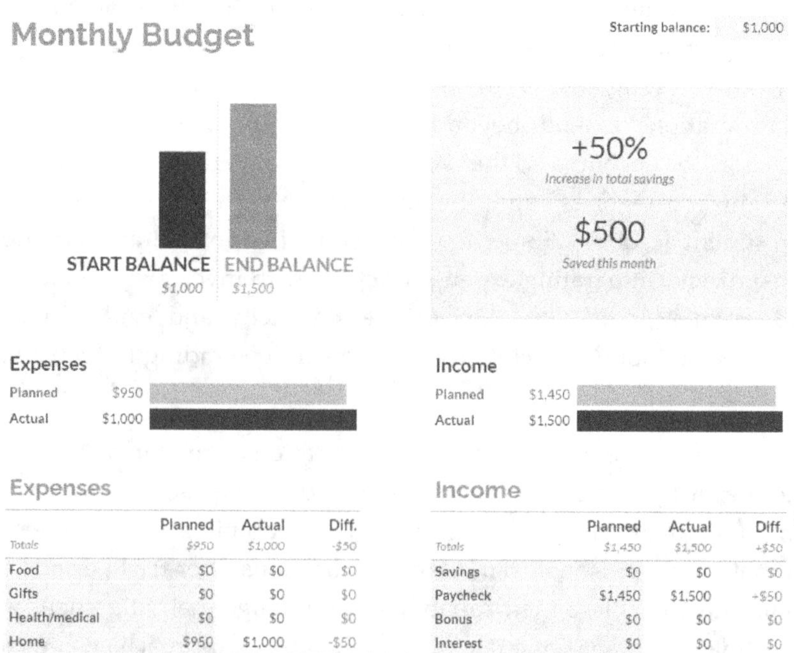

Annual Budget sheet:

Summary

	Jan	Feb	Mar	Apr	May	Jun	Jul	Aug	Sep	Oct	Nov	Dec	*Total*	*Average*
Income	$0	$0	$0	$0	$0	$0	$0	$0	$0	$0	$0	$0	$0	$0
Expenses	$0	$0	$0	$0	$0	$0	$0	$0	$0	$0	$0	$0	$0	$0
Net savings	$0	$0	$0	$0	$0	$0	$0	$0	$0	$0	$0	$0	$0	$0
Ending balance	$5,000	$5,000	$5,000	$5,000	$5,000	$5,000	$5,000	$5,000	$5,000	$5,000	$5,000	$5,000		$5,000

Income

	Jan	Feb	Mar	Apr	May	Jun	Jul	Aug	Sep	Oct	Nov	Dec	*Total*	*Average*
Wages	$0	$0	$0	$0	$0	$0	$0	$0	$0	$0	$0	$0	$0	$0
Other	$0	$0	$0	$0	$0	$0	$0	$0	$0	$0	$0	$0	$0	$0

Expenses

	Jan	Feb	Mar	Apr	May	Jun	Jul	Aug	Sep	Oct	Nov	Dec	*Total*	*Average*
Children	$0	$0	$0	$0	$0	$0	$0	$0	$0	$0	$0	$0	$0	$0
Debt	$0	$0	$0	$0	$0	$0	$0	$0	$0	$0	$0	$0	$0	$0
Education	$0	$0	$0	$0	$0	$0	$0	$0	$0	$0	$0	$0	$0	$0
Entertainment	$0	$0	$0	$0	$0	$0	$0	$0	$0	$0	$0	$0	$0	$0
Everyday	$0	$0	$0	$0	$0	$0	$0	$0	$0	$0	$0	$0	$0	$0
Gifts	$0	$0	$0	$0	$0	$0	$0	$0	$0	$0	$0	$0	$0	$0
Health/medical	$0	$0	$0	$0	$0	$0	$0	$0	$0	$0	$0	$0	$0	$0
Home	$0	$0	$0	$0	$0	$0	$0	$0	$0	$0	$0	$0	$0	$0
Insurance	$0	$0	$0	$0	$0	$0	$0	$0	$0	$0	$0	$0	$0	$0
Pets	$0	$0	$0	$0	$0	$0	$0	$0	$0	$0	$0	$0	$0	$0
Technology	$0	$0	$0	$0	$0	$0	$0	$0	$0	$0	$0	$0	$0	$0

The Balance's Simple 50/30/20 Budget Template

	Monthly Goal	*Monthly Actual*	*Difference*	**Notes**
Gross Monthly Income	$5,000.00	$5,000.00	$0.00	
Needs	$2,500.00	$800.00	$1,700.00	
Wants	$1,500.00	$115.00	$1,385.00	
Savings	$1,000.00	$500.00	$500.00	

Expenses (Monthly)	***Monthly Goal***	***Monthly Actual***	*Difference*	**Notes**
Mortgage/Rent	$800.00	$800.00	$0.00	
Car Payment			$0.00	
Insurance			$0.00	
Auto/Transit			$0.00	
Groceries			$0.00	
Child Care			$0.00	
Loan and CC Repayment			$0.00	
Utilities			$0.00	
Health Care			$0.00	
			$0.00	
			$0.00	
			$0.00	
Personal Care Incl. Clothes			$0.00	
Subscriptions	$50.00	$100.00	-$50.00	
Dining / Entertainment			$0.00	
Vacations			$0.00	
Gift/charity			$0.00	
Home Supples	$50.00	$15.00	$35.00	
Other	$5.00		$5.00	
			$0.00	
			$0.00	
			$0.00	
			$0.00	
Emergency Fund	$150.00	$150.00	$0.00	
Goal #1	$350.00	$350.00	$0.00	
Goal #2			$0.00	

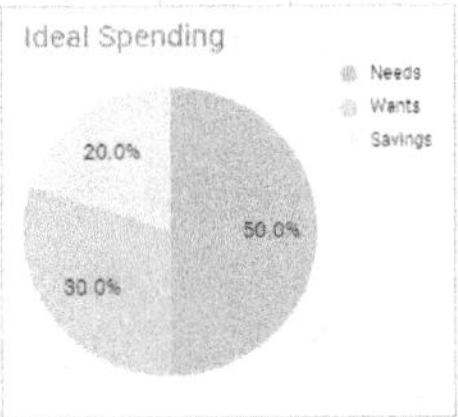

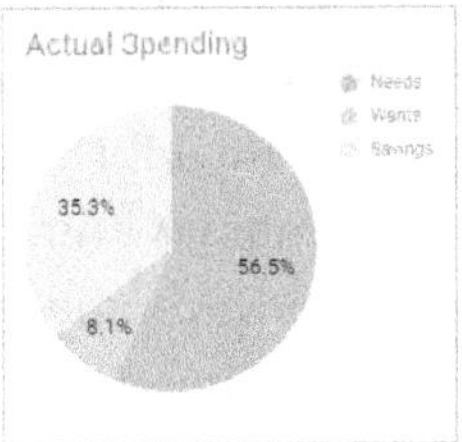

Reference [14]

3.6 SAVINGS GOALS: SETTING AND ACHIEVING THEM

The Role of Savings in Financial Independence

In the world of financial security and independence, savings illuminate the path, acting as both a shield against unforeseen adversities and a ladder toward the realization of long-held aspirations. The essence of savings transcends the mere act of withholding expenditure; it embodies the strategic allocation of resources to fortify one's position against the inevitable vicissitudes of life while paving the way for future prosperity. This dual role underscores the imperative of savings in the architecture of financial well-being, a bulwark against the uncertainties of tomorrow and a huge step towards the fulfillment of personal and financial autonomy.

Setting Smart Savings Goals

Adopting the **SMART** framework in setting savings goals transforms this endeavor from a nebulous ambition to a navigable course.

- Specificity in goal-setting demarcates the boundary between a vague intention and a tangible target, imbuing one's savings efforts with clarity and purpose.
- Measurability introduces a quantifiable metric, a yardstick against which progress can be assessed and celebrated.
- Attainability tempers ambition with realism, ensuring goals remain within the realm of feasibility.
- Relevance ties saving to personal values and aspirations, weaving it into the fabric of one's life narrative.

Lastly, Timeliness imposes a deadline, injecting urgency and focus into the pursuit. This methodology, applied to savings goals, ensures they are not merely wishes cast into the future, but quite actionable objectives grounded in the realities of one's financial landscape.

Strategies to Boost Your Savings

Strategies to amplify the rate of savings pivot on automation and prioritization are embedded into the rhythm of daily life. Automatic transfers, a mechanism that diverts a predetermined portion of income into savings—before expenditures can absorb it—ensure consistency in savings efforts, sidelining human procrastination, rebellion or forgetfulness! The principle of "pay yourself first" elevates savings to a non-negotiable expense, a first claim on one's income rather than a residual afterthought. This approach, reinforced by the Rule of 72 for setting savings goals, (a hypothesis that estimates the time required for savings to double at a given interest rate), offers a blueprint for growth-oriented savings, making visible the exponential potential of consistent, disciplined saving practices.

The cornerstone of a robust savings strategy lies in establishing an emergency fund, a reservoir of liquidity designed to cushion against life's unforeseen financial shocks. This fund acts as a financial moat, safeguarding one's standard of living and long-term savings goals from the disruptive forces of unexpected expenses, be they medical emergencies, sudden unemployment, or urgent home repairs. The priority accorded to this fund, often recommended to cover three to six months of living expenses, underscores its role as a foundational element in the tower of financial security, a first line of defense that preserves one's financial integrity and autonomy in the face of any adversity.

The Role of an Emergency Fund

The terrain of savings is full of obstacles; irregular income streams and the constant pressure of high expenses pose significant challenges. The fluctuation presents a formidable barrier to consistent savings for those whose earnings ebb and flow with the tides of gig work or freelance endeavors. In this context, flexibility and adaptability emerge as allies. These strategies accommodate variability by adjusting savings targets in harmony with income trends, ensuring that saving remains responsive to your financial reality. High expenses, often a reflection of lifestyle choices or the inevitable cost of living, demand a meticulous examination of spending patterns, identifying areas for recalibration or reduction. This scrutiny, coupled with a commitment to living within or below one's means, gradually liberates resources for savings, aligning daily financial decisions with long-term savings objectives.

Overcoming Common Savings Challenges

Pursuing savings goals is proof of one's commitment to financial security and independence. It is a discipline that marries the foresight of planning with the resilience to adapt, a balance between aspiration and pragmatism. Through the application of the SMART framework, the embrace of automation and prioritization, the strategic establishment of an emergency fund, and the navigation of common savings challenges, the act of saving transcends its immediate utility, becoming a cornerstone in the construction of a future marked by financial stability and freedom.

With the groundwork of financial planning laid, and the strategies for achieving savings goals delineated, the journey continues, winding its way toward the intricate world of building and managing credit. This next chapter unfolds as a natural progression, delving into credit scores, debt management, and the strategic use of credit as a tool for financial empowerment—a continuation of the quest for financial independence and well-being.

Reference [9-12] for more tips and resources related to budgeting & budget-tracking apps.

Chapter 3 Action Summary:

1. Take assessment money mindset quizz to understand your current mindset, personal value about money.
2. Evaluate your money mindset and values toward money against Financial Myths vs what you have learned from traditional eduction vs from this book are there any gaps for improvement?
3. Set your personal financial goals, short-term, mid-term, and long-term

4. Download Annual & Monthly budget templates from Google sheet and apply rules 10-10-10-70 or 20-50-30 to generate your own budget & track expenses.
5. download Monthly / Annual expense tracking template from google sheet and start establish your own expense tracking.
6. Setup and start saving for your emergency fund.

CHAPTER FOUR
BUILDING AND MANAGING CREDIT

> *"A good credit score is not just a number, it's a key to unlocking opportunities and achieving financial freedom."*
>
> — UNKNOWN

Imagine standing in front of a vast digital screen, flickering with numbers, terms, and statements—a language all of its own, dictating the ebb and flow of financial opportunities. It is not a scene from a sci-fi movie but a depiction of the modern credit system, an invisible force shaping paths to homeownership, entrepreneurship, and beyond. Grasping this system's language, understanding its signals, and manipulating its levers can unlock doors to financial positions once deemed unattainable.

4.1 CREDIT SCORES DECODED

What Your Credit Score Represents

A credit score is a numerical summary of financial reliability distilled from past debt and payment interactions. Think of it as a trustworthiness badge in the financial realm, like a GPA in academia.

There are three major US credit bureaus:

- TransUnion
- Experian
- Equifax

All three bureaus are regulated by federal laws such as the Fair Credit Reporting Act (FCRA). They collect and maintain credit information on individuals and businesses within the U.S. Each credit bureau may gather information from different sources, such as lenders, creditors, and public records. As a result, your credit report from one bureau may be different from your report from another. Just as a high GPA can open doors to prestigious scholarships and coveted academic opportunities, a strong credit score paves the way for favorable loan terms, lower interest rates, and access to premium financial products. It's a critical determinant in a lender's decision-making process, influencing not just the availability of credit, but the cost of borrowing itself.

Reference [15] how to read your credit report

Factors Affecting Your Credit Score

Several pillars support the structure of a credit score:

- **Payment history (35%):** This accounts for a significant portion of the score. A single late payment can dent this record, echoing in the credit score's computations.
- **Credit utilization ratio (30%):** The ratio of your used credit vs. available credit. Lower ratios signal restraint and financial stability, nudging the score upward.

- **The length of your credit history (15%):** Credit score calculations may consider how long your oldest and most recent accounts have been open. Generally, creditors like to see you have a history of responsibly paying off your credit accounts monthly.
- **The types of accounts (10%):** Showcasing financial experience and a mix of credit types, illustrating versatility in handling credit and recent credit inquiries and indicating the frequency of credit applications. Lenders and creditors like to see that you can manage multiple accounts of different types.
- **The number of accounts you have (10%):** Too many new accounts may impact the length of your credit history.

Reference [13]

Interpreting Your Credit Report

A credit report is a ledger detailing the transactions and behaviors culminating in a credit score. Reading this document requires attention to four sections:

- **Personal information:** Discrepancies in personal information, though seemingly benign, can signal identity errors or fraud.
- **Accounts:** The accounts section, a record list of loans and credit lines, warrants scrutiny for balances and payment history accuracy.
- **Activities Inquiries:** These are when and where credit was applied and should reflect only those you initiated. This document, refreshed periodically, demands regular review to ensure its reflection of your financial narrative remains untarnished.
- **Your Credit Score:** This is your financial score GPA ranking, as detailed below.

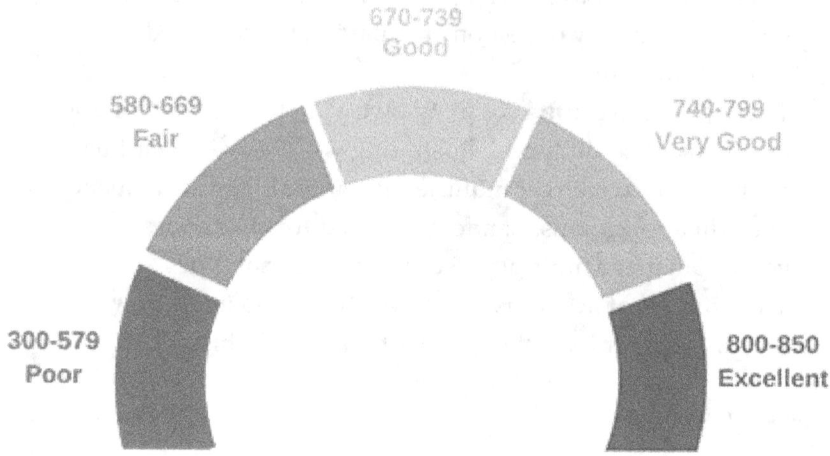

Reference [14]

Anatomy of a Credit Score:

- **Excellent (800 to 850):** Lenders view these borrowers as less risky, so individuals in this range may have an easier time being approved for new credit.
- **Very good (740 to 799):** Very good credit scores reflect frequent positive credit behaviors. Lenders are likely to approve borrowers in this range.
- **Good (670 to 739):** Lenders may think twice before offering new credit to individuals in this range. If approved, borrowers with good credit scores may face higher interest rates than less risky borrowers with higher credit scores.
- **Fair (580 to 669):** Borrowers with credit scores in this range often have a history of poor credit behaviors, which may make lenders reluctant to offer new credit.

- **Poor (300 to 579):** Borrowers with poor credit scores are considered risky and unlikely to be approved by a lender.

Where to obtain your Credit report: Annual Credit Report.com provides one annual free report from all three major bureaus: Transunion, Equifax, and Experian. You can also use other free credit monitor sites like Credit Karma or Credit Sesame. These websites will allow you to view your credit score and provide free credit monitoring services that can help alert you when unusual activities pop up in your credit report.

4.2 ESTABLISHING AND IMPROVE YOUR CREDIT: BEST PRACTICES

Establishing Your Credit Score

As mentioned, an excellent credit score is critical for your journey toward financial independence. For novices on this path, the absence of credit history is like navigating a vessel without a compass—directionless in the vast ocean of credit. The initiation into this realm begins with deliberate steps and careful crafting of one's financial persona in the eyes of potential lenders.

The start of this endeavor has its roots in the strategic acquisition of credit, particularly challenging for those standing at the threshold with no prior history to their name. Below are steps you can take to establish your credit score:

- **Secured credit cards**: The perfect first step for those with no previous credit history. A secured card requires that you deposit up front, usually the same amount as your suggested credit limit. The card works like any other credit card, with on-time payments contributing toward a positive credit history.
- **Student credit cards:** If you qualify, you will likely have to prove that you are enrolled in school, but these cards are

similarly aimed at helping you build credit and establish a credit score.

- **Authorized user:** One way to start building credit without applying for a credit card yourself is to become an authorized user on the credit card account of a parent, spouse, or other family member. As an authorized user, you would receive a credit card with your name on it and reap the benefits of making on-time payments, but the account itself would not be in your name.
- **Co-signer:** A co-signer is a person who agrees to be legally responsible for paying a debt, such as a car or student loan, if the borrower does not pay back the loan as agreed. Having a co-signer may allow you to secure better loan terms or qualify for a loan you might not otherwise get. In turn, you can begin to build credit, but if you fail to pay, your co-signer will be responsible for the debt.
- **Utility and rent payments:** You can also ask your landlord or utility companies to report your on-time payments to the three nationwide consumer reporting agencies. Although these kinds of payments typically don't appear on credit reports, if you know you have a positive payment history, you may be able to have them considered, in your favor.

Unsecured credit, the more conventional form, extends a line of credit without a security deposit, relying instead on the lender's assessment of the borrower's creditworthiness. While this form of credit is more accessible to those with established histories, it remains a distant shore for newcomers. The differentiation between secured and unsecured credit is pivotal, serving as a crossroads where one path offers a guided introduction to credit. In contrast, the other demands a leap of faith from the lender based on the borrower's financial reputation.

Beyond the mechanics of credit-building lies the vigilant watch over one's financial identity, a bastion against fraud and identity theft. The 21st century, with its digital conveniences, also throws shadows where personal information can be stolen, turning the tools of financial advancement into weapons against one's credit standing. Monitoring credit scores has become a shield, alerting individuals to fluctuations and anomalies that hint at more profound issues. Regular perusals of credit reports, a right afforded to consumers, unveil the intricacies of one's credit history, ensuring that each line and account reflects factual accuracy.

In this environment, where credit history forms the bedrock of financial opportunities, establishing a solid foundation is both an art and a science—a balance of strategic decisions, disciplined behavior, and vigilant protection. The initiation into the world of credit, marked by the acquisition of secured or unsecured lines, sets the stage for a journey where every step and decision contribute to the mosaic of one's financial identity. Your financial journey, underscored by the principles of responsibility and protection, unfolds not as a solitary path but as a collective voyage guided by the shared wisdom of many navigators who have charted these waters before.

Improving Your Credit Score

Elevating a credit score is a marathon, not a sprint, requiring strategic actions and patience. The following steps will help to improve your credit score:

- **Pay on time:** Timely payments stand as the most straightforward strategy, directly addressing the most significant component of the score.
    - One of the methods to ensure all monthly bills get paid on time is to set up online bill-pay from a single bank account. It will simplify the monthly accounting in one central place. This way, you can utilize your bank's budget analysis tool to quickly get an overall summary of your monthly spending versus your savings.
    - Gather the due dates of all your monthly bills and pick out one with the earliest due date. Book that date into your calendar reminder and set it as the bill pay date so you can schedule payout for all bills in one shot.
    - Alternatively, you can enable automatic monthly

statement payments from each bill or credit card to ensure they get paid on time. However, with this method, the bank that the fund comes out to pay for all your automatic payments will lose track of what all the payouts are for; thus, its budget analysis tool can't get an accurate summary. It will make your monthly accounting much more complicated.

- **Keep your credit utilization rate low:** Reducing outstanding balances, particularly on revolving credit, can significantly impact credit utilization ratios. It's best to keep your credit utilization rate at or below 30% and ask the credit card company for a credit limit increase.
- **Limit your application for new accounts:** New lines of credit usually lead to a hard inquiry, which can negatively affect your credit score.
- **Diversifying credit types:** Responsibly managing a mix of credit (e.g., installment loans, revolving credit) illustrates to lenders a proficiency in handling various credit forms. These steps, combined with the vigilance against identity theft and errors on credit reports, forge a path to a more robust credit score.
- **Keep old accounts open:** Avoid closing any old paid-off accounts, even if you no longer use them. Keeping the accounts open will help maintain the length of your credit history, which can help improve your credit score.

If you're planning to buy a home but your credit scores aren't where you'd like them to be, consider these steps:

- **Check your credit reports and scores.** Reviewing your credit reports and scores helps familiarize you with your credit history and can help you spot incorrect information that might drag down your credit scores. If you find something you believe may be an error on your credit reports, contact the creditor on the account. It's good practice to review your credit reports and scores regularly.

- **Select your target credit scores.** Setting a specific goal for your credit scores can also be helpful. Generally, you'll have the best chance of approval for a conventional loan with credit scores of 620 or above. Government-backed mortgage options tend to have lower credit score requirements; however, not every homebuyer will qualify for these programs. FHA loans generally require credit scores of at least 580 with a 3.5% down payment or 500 with a 10% down payment. You'll need credit scores of at least 640 for USDA loans, but no down payment is necessary. Although the Veterans Administration (VA) doesn't specify a minimum credit score or down payment to qualify for a VA loan, lenders that issue these loans can set their requirements.
- **Pay your bills on time.** Because your payment history is usually the most influential factor in calculating your credit scores, late payments can significantly negatively impact you. You must keep up with at least the minimum payments on your credit accounts.
- **Raise your credit limits and reduce your debt balance.** Lenders typically prefer that you have a credit utilization ratio of no more than 30%. Using more of your total available credit can suggest you have trouble paying back what you borrow and cannot take on additional debt. If your credit utilization ratio is too high, look at your credit cards, personal lines of credit, HELOCs, and other revolving accounts. If you hold significant debt, work carefully to pay it down. You can also improve your credit utilization ratio by raising one or more of your credit limits. Connect with your credit card provider or lender to request a credit limit increase.
- **Avoid applying for new credit accounts.** While you may think opening a new credit account could positively impact your credit utilization ratio, it's usually better to avoid new accounts if trying to improve your credit scores. Applying for a new line of credit usually triggers a hard inquiry, which appears on

your credit reports to indicate how frequently you have requested new credit. Each hard inquiry has the potential to impact your credit scores negatively.

- **Consider credit counseling to get a handle on significant debt.** If you're carrying significant debt that is negatively impacting your credit scores, a credit counseling service may help. Credit counseling is usually available through nonprofit organizations at low, or no cost. These services provide trained professionals to advise you on the best ways to manage your debt. They could help you create a personalized budget, develop a long-term repayment plan, or even negotiate with your lenders for lower interest rates and more favorable payment terms. Credit counselors can also provide training and best practices to help you establish better credit habits.

This is a practical tool designed to keep your credit score on track, featuring reminders to check credit reports, pay bills on time, review credit utilization, and assess opportunities for credit diversification.

Improving your credit score, like writing a complex piece of music, demands practice, patience, and a keen understanding of the underlying structure. With each responsible financial decision, you compose a melody that plays through your financial life, amplifying opportunities and harmonizing dreams with reality. The journey through the credit system, armed with knowledge and strategic action, is not just about navigating a score, but about unlocking the full range of awaiting financial possibilities.

Reference [16-17] for more tips and resources.

4.3 THE IMPACT OF GOOD VS. BAD CREDIT

The distinction between good and bad credit emerges as a pivotal axis around which a myriad of fiscal opportunities and challenges revolve. A solid credit score, often perceived as a good sign of financial reliability, unlocks a treasure trove of advantages, serving as a key to areas traditionally veiled behind stringent lending criteria. Conversely, the shadow of lousy credit looms, casting a pall over one's financial aspirations, often relegating dreams to the status of unattainable.

The Benefits of a Good Credit Score

The virtues of maintaining an exemplary credit score are manifold:

- A good score secures much lower interest rates that minimize the overall cost of borrowing, and allow you to enjoy more favorable terms of loans, especially with mortgage rates, business loans, and auto loans.
- Beyond the tangible, a strong credit score influences insurance premium costs, and negotiating lower rates is a testament to fiscal responsibility.
- A good credit score also touches the shores of employment opportunities, with certain employers viewing it as a reflection of an individual's reliability and integrity.

The Consequences of Bad Credit

The specter of lousy credit casts long shadows over one's financial power and complicates the trajectory toward fiscal goals.

- The immediate ramifications manifest in borrowing, where higher interest rates emerge as a punitive measure, inflating the cost of loans and eroding the feasibility of financial ventures.
- Financial applications face stricter scrutiny, often resulting in rejection, or the imposition of unfavorable terms. The cascade of consequences further disrupts the housing market, transforming the quest for rental approval into a Herculean task, marred by demands for higher security deposits as landlords hedge against perceived risk.
- Pursuing utilities and telecommunications services becomes fraught with challenges, necessitating deposits as a buffer against a tarnished credit history.

4.4 CREDIT CARDS: FRIEND OR FOE?

In the world of personal finance, credit cards embody both opportunity and peril. Their judicious use can steer a course towards an enhanced financial profile, replete with rewards and an ever-improving credit score. Conversely, a lapse in indiscriminate spending can tether one to a cycle of debt, with serious and far-reaching consequences. You will need insight, discipline, and a strategic approach tailored to your financial profile to use credit cards well.

Maximizing Credit Card Benefits

When utilized with precision, credit cards are powerful tools in augmenting one's financial arsenal. Rewards and cashback programs offer a way to derive tangible benefits from routine transactions. By aligning credit card usage with regular spending patterns—groceries, fuel, or dining out—individuals can accumulate rewards that translate into savings, travel miles, or cashback. This strategic alignment ensures that every dollar spent works doubly, contributing to immediate needs and future gains. Furthermore, the prudent use of credit cards as a method of building credit cannot be overstated. Regular, on-time payments, coupled with a sensible approach to credit utilization, gradually elevate credit scores. Another essential benefit of using a credit card is having a layer of protection from the credit card company for all your good purchases and services, which are unavailable with debit cards or secure cards. With debit cards, you make purchases that are difficult to cancel or refund, the money leaves your bank account straight away. With credit cards, you can dispute the charge or service with far less difficulty, as you don´t pay until the end of the cycle/month.

The Dangers of Credit Card Debt

The shadow credit card debt casts over financial well-being is deep and dark. This form of debt, characterized by high interest rates, can quickly spiral, transforming manageable balances into overwhelming burdens. The ease of transaction—a mere swipe or tap—belies the complexity of escaping the predicament of accruing interest and compounding balances. This hazard underscores the importance of restraint and vigilance in tracking spending, ensuring that usage does not outpace the ability to pay, in full, each billing cycle. For those trapped in credit card debt, strategies such as debt consolidation loans or balance transfer cards offer a reprieve, allowing for debt restructuring under terms that facilitate a return to solvency.

Choosing the Right Credit Card

The selection of a credit card is a decision that demands your introspection and market research. Matching a credit card to one's spending habits and financial goals involves carefully assessing available options and filtering through rewards programs, interest rates, annual fees, and other terms and conditions to find the optimal fit. A card offering travel rewards and no foreign transaction fees might be ideal for frequent travelers. Conversely, for those focused on building credit or managing a fixed budget, a card with a low interest rate and no annual fee may be preferable. This tailored approach ensures that your chosen card *amplifies* financial strategies rather than *undermining* them.

Chapter 4 Action Summary:

1. Get your free copy annual Credit report from *https://www.annualcreditreport.com/index.action*
2. Check:
3. Your Personal information and make sure they are correct
4. Ensure you recognize all the accounts listed in your report
5. Notice all the financial inquiries, banks, credit cards, loans…
6. Check your Credit score and see where you are in the score range
7. Take actions to improve your credit score if needed by applying the steps in section 3.2

CHAPTER FIVE
BUILD YOUR FINANCIAL FREEDOM PLAN

> *"Do not save what is left after spending, but spend what is left after saving."*
>
> — WARREN BUFFETT

Now that we have covered the topic of credit, let's look at building your financial freedom Imagine standing at a crossroads, with every direction promising a different future. One seemingly picks a less-trodden path and veers towards a horizon where the sun sets on financial worries, illuminating a landscape of freedom and choice. The path to financial independence is simple in theory, but intricate in its execution. It is not merely about accumulating wealth, but about crafting a lifestyle that prioritizes autonomy over affluence, where the value of *time* supersedes the worth of *material possessions.*

5.1 THE PATH TO FINANCIAL FREEDOM

Defining Financial Freedom

Financial independence occurs when living expenses can be met without actively trading time for money. It's a state where earned income is optional rather than obligatory, freeing one from the constraints of mandatory work. This liberation allows for a life where decisions are not dictated by financial necessity, but guided by personal fulfillment and purpose.

Steps to Achieve Financial Freedom

Achieving this state involves multifaceted financial strategies:

- Saving your earnings with well established institution that pay you dividend higher than inflation.
- Investing wisely
- Minimizing debt
- Optimize investments/Saving to minimize tax liability
- Establish passive income stream.

The cornerstone of financial independence is establishing an investing and saving plan that applies budgeting rules 10-10-10-70 or 20-50-30 to pay yourself first as soon as you start earning income. Investing these savings becomes the vehicle by which funds can begin to lock in the benefit of compound interest growth. Managing the realms of stocks, bonds, real estate, or alternative investing to generate returns that outpace inflation, will all contribute to a growing nest egg. Concurrently, diligent debt management ensures that liabilities do not anchor one's financial ship, allowing for smoother sailing toward financial independence.

Consider saving on a mundane expense, such as opting for home-brewed coffee over the daily café latte. Extrapolated over the years and invested wisely, this simple choice can translate into quite significant savings, demonstrating how minor lifestyle adjustments can pave the way toward financial independence.

Passive Income Strategies

Generating passive income streams is crucial in this quest. These streams provide financial sustenance without needing you to actively work. Examples include rental income from real estate investments, stock dividends, or earnings from a business that does not require daily involvement. These streams create a financial buffer, ensuring that expenses can be met without dipping into the principal nest egg, thus sustaining financial independence over the long term.

Mindset Shift

Crucial to this path is a shift in mindset, where delayed gratification very much precedes immediate satisfaction. It's about viewing money not as a means for immediate consumption, but as a tool for future freedom. This mindset moves beyond the fleeting joy of material acquisitions to value the enduring satisfaction of autonomy and the ability to pursue passions, unfettered by financial constraints.

Achieving financial independence is like constructing a building, where each brick represents a financial decision, each layer a year of disciplined saving and investing, and the mortar is the passive income that binds the structure together, ensuring its stability.

5.2 BEYOND SAVINGS: EXPLORING INVESTMENT AVENUES

Demystifying Investing

Peering into the world of investments might feel like you are trying to decipher an arcane language with its strange lexicon and rules. Yet, at its core it is simple: investing is the act of allocating resources with the expectation of achieving a future financial return. This fundamental concept unshackles the process from its perceived complexity, inviting individuals to consider investments as tools for building wealth beyond the traditional bastion of savings. To initiate this endeavor, one must understand the various vehicles available—stocks, bonds, mutual funds, and more—each offering unique benefits and risks. The initial step involves recognizing that investing is not at all exclusive to the already affluent; instead, it is accessible to *anyone* willing to act in the financial markets, armed with knowledge and an open-minded willingness to learn.

Diversification is Key

The old axiom, "Don't put all your eggs in one basket" encapsulates the principle of diversification in the investment world. This strategy involves spreading investments across various asset classes (stocks, bonds, real estate) and within asset classes (different sectors, industries, and geographies) to mitigate risk. The logic underpinning diversification is that different assets perform well under various economic conditions; thus, when one investment might underperform—another could thrive, balancing the portfolio's overall performance. A well-diversified portfolio is much like a balanced diet, where the inclusion of varied nutrients (investments) contributes to overall health (financial stability), reducing the risk of malnutrition (financial ruin).

My best resource for investment diversification strategy is ChatGPT. You can ask ChatGPT how to invest assets allocation most effectively. Then, gradually narrow down your prompt to more specific assets, funds, and indexes...For example, I would try, *"What is the most effective long-term investment strategy that best diversifies asset allocation to minimize risk but still earn a good return?* Then follow up with, *"Provide specific investment assets, funds, Indexes in each above category."*

Start Small, Think Big

The notion that substantial capital is requisite for investing is a myth that often discourages novices. In contrast, the advent of financial technology platforms has democratized access to investment opportunities, enabling individuals to commence their investment journey with minimal amounts. The philosophy of starting small advocates for the incremental allocation of funds towards investments that mitigate risk, while fostering a habit of investing, is prevalent in today's investment strategy. Over time, these small contributions accumulate, bolstered by compound interest, illustrating that even modest beginnings can culminate in substantial wealth when nurtured with patience and consistency.

The Power of Compound Interest

Compound interest, often hailed as the eighth wonder of the world, is the process by which money grows exponentially over time as interest earns interest—on itself. To elucidate, consider an initial investment that accrues interest; in the following period, this interest is added to the principal amount, and the *entire sum* earns interest. This cycle continues, leading to growth that accelerates over time. Illustrating this concept demonstrates the staggering difference in outcomes between investing early and delaying. The key to maximizing the benefits of compound interest lies not in the magnitude of the investment—but in the duration, so the adage goes that when it comes to investing, *time in* the market trumps timing the market.

The power of compound interest is illustrated in below table:

- Column#2 shows if you start with just 1 penny and consistently earn double every day then after just 30 days your money will accumulate up to a whooping 53.6 Millions! Isn't that powerful? I bet your jaw is dropping and want to check the table below to validate the number. Although this is in theory, in reality, it's too good to be true to consistently earning double everyday. Yet the power of compound interest is very powerful.
- Column#3 show if you start with $1000 and consistently earn 10% every month. After 8 months your saving will be double, after just a year your saving will accumulate up to $2853 that is 185% earning. Consistently earning 10% per month is not easy in reality, but it is not impossible.
- Column#4 shows that if you start with $10,000 and consistently earn 10% per year, your money will accumulate up to $23,579, which is 136% in interest. This is closer to reality.

# day/month/yr	Compound interest double each day	interest 10% per month	interest 10% per year
1	0.10	1000.00	10000.00
2	0.20	1100.00	11000.00
3	0.40	1210.00	12100.00
4	0.80	1331.00	13310.00
5	1.60	1464.10	14641.00
6	3.20	1610.51	16105.10
7	6.40	1771.56	17715.61
8	12.80	1948.72	19487.17
9	25.60	2143.59	21435.89
10	51.20	2357.95	23579.48
11	102.40	2593.74	25937.42
12	204.80	2853.12	28531.17
13	409.60	3138.43	31384.28
14	819.20	3452.27	34522.71
15	1638.40	3797.50	37974.98
16	3276.80	4177.25	41772.48
17	6553.60	4594.97	45949.73
18	13107.20	5054.47	50544.70
19	26214.40	5559.92	55599.17
20	52428.80	6115.91	61159.09
21	104857.60	6727.50	67275.00
22	209715.20	7400.25	74002.50
23	419430.40	8140.27	81402.75
24	838860.80	8954.30	89543.02
25	1677721.60	9849.73	98497.33
26	3355443.20	10834.71	108347.06
27	6710886.40	11918.18	119181.77
28	13421772.80	13109.99	131099.94
29	26843545.60	14420.99	144209.94
30	53687091.20	15863.09	158630.93

Risk and Return

The interplay between risk and return is a fundamental dynamic in investing, where the potential for higher returns is invariably linked to a higher degree of risk. This relationship dictates that investments with the prospect of yielding substantial gains inherently have greater volatility and the possibility of loss. In contrast, safer investments (e.g., bonds) offer lower returns but more stability. This factor requires an assessment of your risk tolerance. This personal benchmark varies widely among individuals and is influenced by financial goals, investment timelines, and the capacity to endure market fluctuations. Balancing risk and return entails constructing a portfolio that aligns with your risk tolerance while striving to achieve financial objectives, a delicate equilibrium that will guide the allocation of assets.

Common Investment Mistakes to Avoid

Moving in the investment environment is fraught with potential missteps, such as:

- A lack of diversification
- Attempting to time the market
- Succumbing to emotional decision-making
- Investments scam which setup to allow initial easy winning to lure investors to inject more capital for even higher return.

Adherence to a disciplined investment strategy that emphasizes long-term objectives over short-term market movements, and bases decisions on sound financial principles rather than fleeting emotions or market speculation is the antidote to these pitfalls. Investors can sail turbulent waters with equanimity by eschewing the siren call of market timing and maintaining a steadfast focus on the horizon.

Understanding the Markets

The financial markets, a pulsating ecosystem of buyers and sellers, are arenas where securities are traded, and values are in constant flux, influenced by a myriad of factors—from global economic indicators to company-specific news. Gaining a rudimentary understanding of how these markets operate—acknowledging the cyclical nature of economies, recognizing the impact of interest rates, and deciphering the signals sent by market indices—equips investors (such as maybe you!) with the context needed to make informed decisions. While not exhaustive, this knowledge serves as a compass, guiding investors through the ebbs and flows of market dynamics.

Popular Type of Investments and Their Tax implication:

There are so many types of different investments in today's market. The scope of this book is not intended to cover all the investment types; instead, I will only focus on the fundamental concept of investment. Let group investments into the following categories:

1. Short-term Investments with Tax now:

Objective: Liquidity and flexible funds access. These are individual brokerage accounts that trade Stocks, Options, bonds, ETFs (Exchange Traded Funds), Index funds, and mutual funds year-round.

Advantage:

- There is no limitation on how much $ you can invest.
- There is no restriction on when you can contribute or withdraw $.
- Flexible, high potential reward (depends on individual investor skills & knowledge)

Disadvantage:

- Higher risk of losing due to higher volatility
- Get taxed when investment gets sold & gain is recognized at year-end tax filing.

2. Immediate-term investments with Tax now:

(Non-government employer investment benefit, popular with High-tech Companies)

Objective: Investing in an employer's stock incentive programs, such as ESPP (Employee Stock Purchase Plan) and RSU (Restrict Stock Unit) bonus awards, these investments usually guarantee profit

Advantage:

- Getting employer stock as a bonus award (RSU) quarterly, annually
- Purchase company stock at a discount price (usually 15% discount) bi-yearly
- Profit return is almost guaranteed (unless the employer's stock is losing badly and quickly).

Disadvantage:

- Can only invest or access to money Quarterly or bi-yearly
- Have a cap limit on how much you can invest
- The company will deduct tax right away at the time investment gets sold & gain is recognized.

3. Long-term Investments with Tax-deferred:

Objective: Long-term investment gain with contribution tax deductible and free matching from employer's retirement accounts 401K / 403b or IRA (individual retirement account).

Advantage:

- Non-government employers usually offer free matching to employee's 401K retirement accounts, up to 3%—6% of the paycheck, in addition to employee contributing.
- Employee contributions to these accounts are tax-deductible; thus, more money is invested, which can boost total investment growth faster.
- Investing in these accounts will help establish a consistent automatic investment system that takes advantage of compound interest and a lower investment cost average.
- Account owners can borrow from their 401K account (usually maximum 50K, depend on the employer's policy) to buy a primary home, personal loan, or hardship with loan interest going back into the owner's account. This is a good source for intermediate emergency funds.

Disadvantage:

- Have a cap limit on how much money you can put in per year.
- You must have earned income to qualify, and if you withdraw before you are 59 ½ years old, there is a 10% penalty on top of the ordinary tax on the principal and all accumulated gain from the account.

- There is a high risk that the tax rate will increase during your retirement when you need to withdraw from these accounts, and you will end up paying higher taxes.
- Withdrawals from these accounts are taxable income at retirement; thus, they will be counted toward provisional income (combined of earned income and Social Security Income). If this combined income is above the IRS allow limits (refer to reference 18 below for IRS's limits), it could trigger tax on your Social Security benefit (50% up to 85% of your SS benefit could be count as taxable income). *[Reference-18]*

4. Long-term Investments with Tax-Free:

Objective: Long-term gain investment with no tax liability. These are retirement accounts such as Roth IRA, Roth 401K, HSA, 529, ESAs, Municipal bonds, Life Insurance Cash account investment, and treasury bonds.

Advantage:

- Tax-free with all long-term gain accumulated in this account, as long as the account is established for 5 years or longer and withdrawn after you are 59 ½.
- Worry-free from any future tax rate increase since tax has no impact on these accounts.
- Systematic enforcement of consistent automatic investment year-round to maximize compound interest and lower investment cost average.
- Income withdrawals from these accounts at retirement will not be counted as combined income (provisional income), thus they will not impact social security benefit.[Reference-18]

Disadvantage:

- The contribution money is after tax (not tax-deductible, except HSAs and ESAs), resulting in less investment capital at the start.

- Have a cap limit of how much $ you can put in per year.(Roth IRA/401K, HSA, 529)
- You must have earned income to qualify, and if you withdraw before you are 59 ½, there is a 10% penalty on top of the ordinary tax on the principal and all accumulated gain from the account.

5. Alternative Investments

Beyond the traditional arenas of stocks and bonds lie alternative investments, avenues that offer the potential for diversification and unique benefits:

Real estate investments, whether through direct property ownership, fix and flip, or real estate investment trusts (REITs), offer tangible assets and the prospect of rental income.

Tax lien and tax deed investments provide a path to acquiring property or earning interest guarantee minimum of 5% up to between 10%-20%. Earning interest rate vary from state to state.

Life insurance with cash account investment policy (Indexed Universal Life Insurance; IUL), a combined life insurance financial death benefit protection, guaranteed investment return, tax-free investment earnings, cash accessibility and flexibility, and long-term care (LTC) rider under one umbrella insurance policy. This alternative investment vehicle could be ideal for your investment diversification and protection with multiple benefits as below:

- Guaranteed a minimum positive interest rate of return in bear market years and can be up to Max. cap of 15% return in bull market years. This feature provides you peace of mind, knowing your investment is guaranteed gain.
- Tax-free earning is one significant advantage of this investment. The cash value is invested in the S&P 500 or Global market index, ensuring low fees and low risk. This tax-efficient structure can significantly enhance your investment returns.

- Another unique aspect of this alternative investment is its loan for cash withdrawals feature which allow you to take your money out from this account at any time for any purpose without any penalty, up to 90% of the total cash value, and without incurring investment gain tax. Some policies even credit the loan interest back into your own account. It's like borrowing from your 401K retirement account but with much lower fees and interest rates.
- Refer to *[Reference 19-20]* for more details about IUL.

The above-mentioned alternative investments are just few and each have their own set of considerations and risk profiles. You should consult with a professional expert to expand the horizon of investment options, enabling the construction of a portfolio that resonates with your individual preferences and financial goals.

In the multifaceted world of investments, the journey from novice to informed investor is marked by a continuous quest for knowledge, a disciplined approach to risk management, and a commitment to long-term financial objectives. This exploration, far from being a solitary endeavor, is a passage forged by learning from missteps, celebrating milestones, and persistently pursuing the growth of one's financial acumen.

Reference[21-23] for additional investment strategies and financial education resources

5.3 UNDERSTANDING TAXES: BASICS FOR YOUNG ADULTS

Few tasks are as universally daunting (yet undeniably crucial) in the labyrinth of adult responsibilities as complying with the complexities of taxes. For many young adults, the transition from the simplicity of a teenager's financial landscape to the intricate web of personal finance in adulthood is marked by their first encounter with tax filing. While often met with apprehension, this rite of passage serves as a cornerstone in the building of financial literacy, laying the groundwork for your future where informed decisions lead to optimized financial outcomes.

Navigating Tax Filing

At its inception, the process of filing taxes appears cloaked in a veil of complexity, a puzzle where each piece represents a different document, deduction, or deadline. However, when approached with methodical precision, this task can be unfolded into some manageable steps:

- Gathering essential documents—W-2 forms from employers
- 1099 forms for independent contractors or self-employment income
- 1099-INT / DIV records of any earned interest savings or dividends
- Records and transactions of all saving, investments profit/loss (stock, bond, real estate) for the year
- Mortgage loan interest paid form 1098 and property tax paid (if there is a home mortgage)

These documents are the bedrock upon which your USA tax return is constructed, each entry a thread in the tapestry of your financial year.

Equally important is an awareness of deadlines, with April 15th etched in the collective consciousness as the day by which returns must be submitted to avoid penalties. Yet, for those who need more time, the Internal Revenue Service (IRS) offers the option of filing for an extension until Oct. 15th. You have to file extension form and have to figure out your estimate tax liabilities and pay it by the original due date, April 15th.

Tax Deductions and Credits

Astute knowledge translates directly into financial savings with regard to tax deductions and credits. Deductions reduce the amount of income on which one is taxed, such as student loan interest deductions, or contributions to retirement accounts. These deductions can significantly lower taxable income, thereby reducing overall tax liability.

In parallel, tax credits directly reduce the tax owed, with the Earned Income Tax Credit (EITC) and the American Opportunity Tax Credit (AOTC) standing as pillars for those who qualify, particularly benefiting low to moderate-income individuals and students. An understanding of these fiscal tools ensures compliance with tax laws and actively works to minimize the tax burden, a strategic element in maximizing one's financial resources.

State vs. Federal Taxes

The distinction between US state and federal taxes is a fundamental aspect of the tax landscape, each governed by its own set of rules and rates. Federal taxes, collected by the IRS, are consistent across the United States, funding national programs and services. In contrast, state taxes vary widely, with each state setting its rates and determining the applicability of taxes on income, property, and sales. This divergence necessitates a dual approach to tax preparation. The implications of these taxes on personal finances are profound, influencing everything from the net income realized to the strategic consideration of where to actually live and work.

The landscape of taxes, with its myriad pathways and potential pitfalls, demands a proactive and well-informed approach. For young adults entering this arena, the mastery of tax filing basics, the strategic utilization of deductions and credits, the understanding of state versus federal taxes, and the implementation of long-term tax planning strategies are an important foundation upon which financial stability and growth are built. Though initially challenging to construct, this foundation becomes a bastion of knowledge that supports a lifetime of informed financial decisions. And there are qualified tax advisors and agents to help you file your annual return.

[Reference 25] for additional tax resources knowledge.

5.4 DEBT MANAGEMENT: STRATEGIES FOR A DEBT-FREE LIFE

Debt often plays the antagonist in personal finance, a formidable force capable of derailing even the most meticulously crafted financial plans.

Yet, with astute management and a proactive stance, this adversary can be tamed, morphing from a source of financial strain into a manageable element of one's fiscal landscape. Realizing the goal of a debt-free existence requires a deep dive into the nature of debt, strategic repayment tactics, and a steadfast commitment to positive habits that fortify against future indebtedness.

Understanding Different Types of Debt

In the financial ecosystem, debt proliferates in a myriad of forms, each bearing distinct characteristics and implications for your financial health. At the heart of this lies the distinction between "good debt" and "bad debt," this difference hinges on the potential of the incurred debt to enhance, or diminish, one's financial foundation. Good debt, (epitomized by student loans or mortgages), is characterized by its potential to foster wealth generation, or elevate one's earning capacity. These debts, often accompanied by favorable terms and lower interest rates, are investments in future financial stability and growth.

In contrast, bad debt, typically embodied by high-interest credit card balances or payday loans, offers no such potential for financial advancement. Instead, it erodes wealth, its excessive costs as a drain on resources, and a barrier to financial goals.

Debt Repayment Strategies

The path to liberating yourself from the shackles of debt is paved with strategic repayment plans, each tailored to individual circumstances and psychological makeup. The Snowball Method, emphasizing the psychological momentum gained from paying off smaller debts first, advocates for listing debts from smallest to largest and directing extra payments toward the smallest balance while maintaining minimum payments on others. This strategy, celebrated for its motivational benefits, creates a cascade of victories that propel you toward the ultimate goal of total debt elimination.

Conversely, the Avalanche Method, guided by financial efficiency, prioritizes debts with the highest interest rates, targeting the most expensive debts first, and progressing to those with lower rates. This approach, while potentially less immediately gratifying than the Snowball Method, minimizes the overall interest paid, optimizing financial resources for debt reduction.

I personally prefer the Avalance Method, which helps to reduce the overall interest paid. However, the choice between these tactics depends on personal preference, financial situation, and psychological resilience, with the optimal strategy sustaining motivation (and adherence) over time.

Avoiding Common Debt Traps

Forewarned is forearmed in the battle against debt, where awareness of common pitfalls plays a crucial role in safeguarding your financial health. With their seductive offers and ease of use, **high-interest credit cards** often lure individuals into a vortex of compounding debt, the casual convenience of swiping eclipsing the reality of repayment terms and interest rates. Similarly, **payday loans,** presenting a quick fix to immediate cash shortfalls, trap borrowers in cycles of debt characterized by *astronomical* interest rates and fees.

The defense against such traps lies in vigilance, education, and a commitment to understanding financial products' terms and long-term implications before formal engagement. It extends to cultivating a mindset that prioritizes inquiry and skepticism over impulsivity, ensuring that decisions are made with a *full* comprehension of their potential impact on your finances.

Building a Debt-Free Future

Central to building a fiscally responsible debt-free existence is the aforementioned budgeting—a disciplined approach to mapping out income and expenditure that ensures living within your means.

Parallel to budgeting is the emphasis on saving, creating a financial buffer that protects against the need to go into debt in response to unforeseen expenses. This commitment to building and maintaining an emergency fund is a testament to the principle of preparedness—a bulwark against life's uncertainties.

Investing, too, plays a pivotal role in the quest for a debt-free existence, offering a means to grow wealth beyond the limitations of savings. Through prudent and strategic investment decisions, individuals can generate returns that outpace inflation, contributing to a financial base that supports not just the elimination of existing debt, but the prevention of any future debt.

Managing debt effectively and forging a path to a debt-free life is marked by the need for a deep understanding of the types of debt, the implementation of strategic repayment plans, and the cultivation of habits that prevent future indebtedness. It is a journey characterized not by quick fixes—but by sustained effort, discipline, and a commitment to ongoing financial education and growth. Through this multifaceted approach, the goal of financial freedom becomes an achievable reality.

[Reference 26] for additional resources.

5.5 REAL ESTATE BASICS: TO RENT OR TO BUY?

To plant seeds in your plot of earth or to navigate the flexibility of renting is a pivotal financial decision many of us face. Influenced by a range of personal priorities, financial realities, and future aspirations, this choice is a cornerstone of adult life. On the one hand, the allure of homeownership promises permanence, equity, and a truly personal domain. On the other, renting offers flexibility, minimal responsibility, and freedom from the unpredictable burdens of inevitable property maintenance activity.

Pros and Cons of Renting vs. Buying

Renting, for many, presents a practical solution in periods of life characterized by transition or uncertainty. The absence of maintenance obligations, the flexibility to relocate with relative ease, and the freedom from property taxes and homeowners' insurance are all feathers in the cap of renting. Yet, on this path you also walk hand in hand with potential increases in rental rates, restrictions on personalization of the living space, and the stark reality that monthly payments build equity for the landlord—not you, the tenant.

Conversely, buying a home builds equity with each mortgage payment, a tangible asset that traditionally appreciates over time. The pride of homeownership is interwoven with the autonomy to modify one's home to mirror personal tastes and needs. However, this route demands the readiness to shoulder maintenance costs, property taxes, and potentially higher upfront costs, including the down payment.

The decision between these two housing solutions impacts not just your lifestyle but the long-term financial landscape of your life.

Understanding Mortgages

Mortgages usually stand as a gatekeeper to homeownership, a financial mechanism that demands careful consideration while enabling the purchase of a home. Mortgages (essentially loans secured by the property itself), unravel in various types designed to cater to the diverse needs of borrowers. Fixed-rate mortgages, with their unchanging interest rates over the life of the loan, offer a harbor of predictability in the turbulence of financial markets. Conversely, adjustable-rate mortgages (ARMs) change their interest rates in alignment with market trends—a double-edged sword that can offer lower initial rates, but carries the risk of future increases.

Qualifying for either of these loans will mandate a thorough audit of one's financial health, scrutinizing credit scores, income stability, and debt-to-income ratios. In their role as custodians of capital, lenders seek assurance in the borrower's ability to repay, making the qualification process a reflection of your financial responsibility and readiness for the commitments of homeownership.

Real Estate as an Investment

Beyond its role as a human shelter, real estate emerges as a formidable player in investment strategies. Its dual nature, serving as a tangible asset and a potential source of passive income through rental payments, positions it in a special place in the investment landscape. The allure of real estate investment lies in its potential for appreciation, tax advantages, and the leverage afforded by mortgage financing, allowing for the control of a significant asset with a fraction of its value (often 20% down payment) paid upfront.

Yet, this avenue is clearly not without its challenges. The responsibilities of a landlord, the unpredictability of property values, and the illiquidity of real estate assets demand a strategic approach, balancing potential returns against the realities of property management and market fluctuations. The decision to incorporate real estate into one's investment portfolio thus hinges on a careful assessment of these factors, weighing risks and rewards, aiming for financial growth and stability.

In the grand scheme of personal finance, the decision to rent or buy, the understanding of mortgages, the steps involved in purchasing a home, and considering real estate as an investment are all part of the story of your financial planning. Each choice, and each strategy contributes to the mosaic of one's financial future, reflecting individual priorities, circumstances, and aspirations.

5.6 FINANCIAL PLANNING FOR LIFE EVENTS: MARRIAGE, CHILDREN, AND BEYOND

Financial Considerations for Marriage

When two lives join in matrimony, so do their financial lives, knitting together shares of assets, debts, and fiscal goals. Managing this merger necessitates open dialogue, where expectations about money management, spending habits, and financial aspirations are laid bare, fostering a foundation of transparency and mutual understanding.

Couples might find solace in establishing joint accounts for household expenses while maintaining individual accounts for personal spending, a hybrid approach that honors collective responsibility as well as personal autonomy. Setting shared goals, whether for purchasing a home, planning vacations, or saving for retirement, becomes a collaborative endeavor, with each partner contributing to a singular, shared vision that encapsulates both of their dreams.

Crafting a unified financial strategy also involves harmonizing debt management plans, where existing liabilities are addressed with concerted effort, and future borrowing is approached with caution, ensuring that the couple's financial health remains robust. Previously tailored to individual needs, insurance policies now demand reevaluation, with considerations for spousal benefits and the implications of merging health, life, and property insurance plans.

This comprehensive approach to financial planning within marriage underscores the importance of adaptability, communication, and shared objectives. It guides couples as they enjoy the complexities of married life with a good sense of financial savvy and resilience.

Planning for Children

Having a baby introduces a kaleidoscope of joy, challenges, and significant financial implications, starting from pregnancy to many years of education, and even beyond. Anticipating the costs associated with childbirth and the ensuing care requires a proactive stance, with savings plans tailored to cover medical expenses, maternity/paternity leave, and the myriad costs of newborn necessities. This foresight extends into childcare, a considerable expense that demands strategic planning, whether through budget adjustments, exploring flexible work arrangements, or considering family support networks.

Plan ahead to ensure you have excellent medical health insurance for your childbirth. You should enroll in your Medical health benefit in the prior year of your childbirth. Select a health plan that requires a low deductible, low co-pay, and minimal total out-of-pocket cost. That way, you can avoid the stress and headache of having to pay a high deductible and co-pay to the hospital for your baby's delivery.

For childcare expenses, you should enroll in a Flexible Saving Account (FSA) benefit your employer offers to take advantage of tax-deductible for your childcare expenses. However, the funds you send into an FSA account must be spent that same year; otherwise, it could be forfeited.

As a result, you need to estimate the total childcare expenses you will be paying for that year so that you can send in just enough into your FSA account to avoid being forfeited. Notice that most employers have an extension for FSA spending into the following year, so you should check and verify with your health benefit admin.

The horizon of financial planning for children stretches far into the future, with education savings plans taking a prominent place in parental considerations. Vehicles such as 529 plans offer a tax-advantaged method of saving for college, allowing parents to invest in their child's educational future while benefiting from tax breaks and potential growth over time. However, there are also disadvantages to the 529 plan.

Consider the advantages vs. disadvantages of a 529 plan and compare them with aforementioned alternative investments. Setup an appointment with each plan to have their representative share with you a more detail about each plan.

529 ADVANTAGES:

1. Tax Benefits:

- *Tax-Free Growth*: Earnings in a 529 plan grow federal tax-free and will not be taxed when the money is withdrawn for qualified education expenses.
- *State Tax Benefits*: Many states offer state tax deductions or credits for contributions to a 529 plan.

DISADVANTAGES:

1. Penalties for Non-Qualified Withdrawals:

- *Taxes and Penalties*: If the money is not used for qualified education expenses, the earnings portion of the withdrawal will be subject to income tax and a 10% penalty.

2. Limited Investment Choices:

- *Investment Options*: Investment options are typically limited to the portfolios offered by the plan, which may not suit all investors' preferences.

3. Fees:

- *Plan Fees*: Some 529 plans may have higher fees and expenses compared to other investment vehicles.

4. State-Specific Plans:

- *Variation in Benefits*: The tax benefits and other advantages can vary significantly from state to state, influencing which plan is most beneficial.

5. Impact on Financial Aid:

- *Beneficiary Impact*: While generally favorable, having a 529 plan could still impact financial aid eligibility to a certain extent in some cases.

6. Changing Tax Laws:

- *Legislative Risk*: Tax benefits and rules regarding 529 plans are subject to change with new legislation, which could affect their advantages.

[Reference 27] for additional resource reference.

Instilling in children a sense of financial literacy is a crucial part of their upbringing, equipping them with the knowledge and habits necessary to run their own finances with confidence and insight.

Estate Planning Essentials

Often shrouded in misconceptions of complexity and discomfort, estate planning emerges as a critical component of comprehensive financial planning. This ensures that your family's primary financial source is protected, avoids probate (a lengthy and costly process to wait for court and attorney process to go through all your assets and determine how and what assets can be distributed to your love one), and minimizes the burden and stress to family and your loved one in the event you are no longer there for them. At its core, estate planning involves the creation of a will or living trust. These legal documents delineate the distribution of assets, guardianship of minor children, and execution of final wishes.

Living Trusts, serving as vehicles for the management and distribution of assets, offer an additional layer of control and flexibility, allowing for the specification of how and when assets are to be allocated to beneficiaries to avoid costly probate process.

Healthcare directives and powers of attorney stand as sentinels of personal autonomy, guiding medical and financial decisions in the event of incapacity. These instruments ensure that one's preferences regarding healthcare and the management of financial affairs are respected, even without the ability to personally communicate those wishes. Far from being a morbid contemplation, estate planning is an act of love and responsibility—safeguarding one's family from uncertainty and conflict while honoring personal values and priorities.

Most employers offer legal service benefits that subside or co-pay the initial setup cost of estate planning. You should sign up for this legal service at your company's annual benefit enrollment for the year you plan to set up your estate planning plan to save on the setup cost.

5.7 INSURANCE: WHAT YOU NEED AND WHY

Insurance, with its varied forms and functions, serves as protection against negative and unforeseen events, offering a semblance of stability amidst the many uncertainties that color human existence. Far from being just a contractual obligation, insurance is a strategic component of comprehensive financial planning—safeguarding the hard-earned assets and fiscal well-being of individuals and families alike.

Types of Insurance

Myriad insurance policies cater to individuals' divergent needs and risks.

Health insurance, a cornerstone of personal welfare, mitigates the financial impact of medical expenses, from routine check-ups to unexpected health emergencies. It ensures access to necessary care without the debilitating burden of out-of-pocket costs.

Life insurance, spanning the term to whole life policies, is a financial lifeline for beneficiaries after a policyholder's demise. It provides a solution for final expenses, outstanding debts, financial burdens, and ongoing living costs to help alleviate pain and suffering for loved ones and help them move forward with peace and comfort.

Auto insurance, mandated by law in many jurisdictions, shields drivers from the financial repercussions of accidents, covering repair costs, medical expenses, and liability claims.

Meanwhile, homeowner's and renter's insurance protect the sanctity of your home, offering coverage for property damage, loss of personal belongings, and liability for injuries occurring on the premises.

These kinds of insurance policies, integral to a well-rounded financial strategy, act as a safeguard, transforming potential financial catastrophes into much more manageable incidents.

Evaluating Insurance Needs

Figuring out your needs for insurance is a personal matter, reflecting individual circumstances, life stages, and risk tolerance. Young adults, embarking on their professional journeys, may prioritize health insurance and renter's policies, while families might focus on life and homeowner's insurance. The assessment hinges on thoroughly evaluating assets, potential liabilities, and the financial impact of unforeseen events. Consideration of plans, such as starting a family or purchasing a home, further informs this evaluation.

Understanding Policy Terms

The vocabulary of insurance, with terms like deductibles, premiums, coverage limits, and exclusions, often presents quite a barrier to the uninitiated. Deductibles, the out-of-pocket costs before insurance takes effect, and premiums, the regular insurance coverage payments, constitute your financial commitment. Coverage limits set the maximum amount an insurer will pay for a claim, while exclusions detail what is *not* covered under the policy. Mastery of such terms and an understanding of policy specifics empowers you to make informed decisions about your (inevitable) insurance.

Shopping for Insurance

The search for appropriate insurance coverage demands a strategic approach. Comparison shopping, leveraging online tools and resources, allows individuals to juxtapose policies based on coverage, costs, and customer reviews. Inquiries about discounts for bundling policies, maintaining a clean driving record, or installing home security systems can yield substantial savings. Independent insurance agents offer personalized guidance, drawing on their expertise to match personal needs with suitable policies. Taking a proactive approach, doing diligent research, and making informed inquiries will give you optimal insurance coverage at competitive rates. You could use moodys.com or Standard & Poor's (link below) to research credit ratings for an insurance brokerage firm to ensure they have a good, reputable credit rating and are reliable. Refer to the Investopedia link below to understand more about what credit rating is and how it is used.

https://www.moodys.com/researchandratings/market-segment/insurance/insurance-brokerage/005009002?tb=0

https://www.investopedia.com/terms/c/creditrating.asp

INDEX LIFE INSURANCE FOR FINANCIAL PROTECTION, EMERGENCY FUND, AND DIVERSIFY YOUR INVESTMENT

As aforementioned, Indexed Universal Life (IUL) insurance is a hybrid that melds the protective assurances of life insurance with the growth potential of equity index investments tax-fee earnings. IUL policies, characterized by their flexibility in premiums and increased death benefits, allocate a portion of the paid premium to a cash value account linked to a stock market index. The unique structure of IUL policies shields the cash value from market downturns with a guaranteed minimum return while allowing for participation in market upswings. Below are the advantages vs disadvantages of an IUL Insurance policy:

Advantages:

1. Tax Benefits:

- *Tax-Deferred Growth:* The cash value of an IUL grows on a tax-deferred basis. This means you don't pay taxes on the earnings until you withdraw them.
- *Tax-Free Loans*: Policyholders can take out loans against the cash value or withdraw. Loans are typically tax-free, provided the policy is not surrendered.

2. Flexible Premiums:

- *Adjustable Payments:* Policyholders have the flexibility to adjust premium payments within certain limits, allowing them to pay more in good financial times and less when money is tight.

3. Potential for Higher Returns:

- *Market-Linked Growth*: The cash value is linked to the S&P 500 or Global market index. It offers low risk, low fees, and potentially higher returns than traditional whole-life policies without the direct risk of investing in the stock market.

4. Death Benefit:

- *Flexible Death Benefit:* IUL policies offer the flexibility to adjust the death benefit as your needs change over time.
- *Death Benefit Increase*: Policyholders have the option to choose an increase in death benefit so that the total benefit payout will be a combination of the policy death benefit plus total cash value.

5. No Direct Stock Market Risk:

- *Index-Linked:* Since the cash value is not directly invested in the stock market, policyholders do not suffer direct losses if the market performs poorly.

6. Accessibility to Cash Value:

- *Flexibility cash access and low fees:* Cash in the policy can be borrowed out at any time, up to 90% of the total cash value in the account, and can be used for any purpose without restriction or penalty. Loan fees and interest are very low, and some policies even offer credit back the loan interest into the policyholder's account.

Disadvantages:

1. Costs and Fees:

- *High Fees:* IULs can have higher fees and charges than other types of life insurance, including administrative fees, mortality charges, and the cost of insurance.
- *Surrender Charges:* If you decide to surrender the policy early, you may incur significant surrender charges, which will reduce the amount you receive.

2. Caps limit on earning:

- *Growth Limits*: The potential returns on the cash value investment are subject to caps (maximum return limits), usually only up to 15%. These can limit the cash value's growth.

With a multitude of benefits and advantages, IUL insurance stands out as a compelling component of a diversified investment portfolio. It not only provides family financial protection but also serves as a tax-advantaged savings vehicle with the potential for significant cash accumulation. Whether you're looking to supplement your retirement savings, fund future expenses, establish an emergency fund, or leave a financial legacy, IULs offer a strategic option that combines the benefits of insurance and investment in a single financial instrument. Understanding the intricacies of IUL policies, from the calculation of interest credits to the implications of withdrawal and loans against the cash value, is crucial to ensure that this sophisticated financial tool aligns with your overall strategy and objectives.

Insurance is integral to your holistic financial plan, from the advisable coverage provided by health, life, auto, and homeowner's/renter's insurance to the innovative investment opportunities IULs offer. Armed with knowledge and strategic foresight, steering through this domain enables you to secure your financial assets *and* peace of mind.

Refer to *[Reference 19-20]* for additional resources.

5.8 RETIREMENT PLANNING: STARTING EARLY IN YOUR 20S—FOR A SECURE FUTURE

Importance of Early Planning

In life's regular and important financial considerations, few topics are as critical (yet often neglected) as retirement planning. The allure of immediate gratification frequently overshadows the prudent—albeit less thrilling—practice of early retirement preparation. However, those who begin to take care of this subject in their 20s find themselves on a shorter path to achieve financial freedom much earlier, where work becomes *optional* rather than mandatory.

Essential Components For Retirement Planning:

1. Assessing Retirement Needs:

- *Income Requirements:* Estimate how much income you'll need annually during retirement, considering living expenses, healthcare, travel, and leisure activities. This can be based on your current expenses adjusted for inflation and lifestyle changes.

  A method that I use for a rough estimate of retirement income required is as follows:

  i. Start with your current monthly take-home after tax deductions. Let's say 10,000/month is your current expense (for easy calculation).
  ii. How many years before your retirement? Let say 45yrs (20s now)
  iii. Typically, total expense at retirement is estimated to be between 80% and 70% of the current lifestyle expenses. Let's use 70%, you would need 7,000 / month at retirement (10,000 x 70%)
  iv. Estimate the inflation impact; let's take an average inflation rate of 3%. Apply rule 72 (72 / 3 is 24). This means you will need to double the amount every 24 years to beat inflation. As a result, when you retire at age 65, you would need roughly 25,000/month to beat inflation and maintain 70% of your current lifestyle. ($7000/month currently, 24 years later would need $14,000/month, another 21 years would need ~ $25,000/month).

v. You need to establish multiple streams of retirement investments now to invest and accumulate compound interest for your retirement income. The sooner, the better.

- *Longevity Risk*: Plan for a longer lifespan to ensure your savings last throughout your retirement years. With increasing life expectancy, it's crucial to have sufficient funds to cover potentially lengthy retirement periods.

2. Sources of Retirement Income:

- *Social Security*: Understand your Social Security benefits and the optimal time to start taking them to maximize your payout.
- *Pensions*: If you have a pension, understand its benefits and the payout options available to you.
- *Savings and Investments tax-deferred*: Plan your investment in these accounts, 401K/403b, IRAs to get benefits of contribution tax deductible, investment gain tax-deferred, and free employer's matching contributions. You must determine the contributions and growth rates needed to meet your retirement number. However, be aware these investment accounts also have their disadvantages. As mentioned above in the "Popular Type of Investment" section, these are taxable & tax-deferred incomes at retirement. They will be counted as provisional income, which could trigger taxable income on your Social Security benefit (from 50% and up to 85% of your Social Security benefit will be counted as taxable income) if the amount withdrawn from these accounts combined with 50% of your SS benefit plus all other dividends incomes pass above IRS allow limits. As a result, having too much cash in these tax-deferred accounts at your retirement might not always be beneficial.
- *Investments in Tax-free retirement income*: Take control of your financial future by setting up and contributing to Roth IRA/Roth 401K early. These options offer the flexibility of tax-

free investment gains and withdrawals without worrying about tax-rate increases or impacting your social security benefit at retirement. This flexibility allows you to adapt your financial strategy to changing circumstances, giving you the power to secure your retirement.

- *Index Universal Life Insurance cash value Investment for retirement:* Strengthen your investment portfolio by diversifying with an IUL. This strategy offers financial protection, guaranteed investment gain, and a tax-free withdrawal feature. I highly recommend you read or listen to the audible book *"Look Before You LIRP"* by David McKnight (#ad Scan the QR code below to get it from Amazon) to gain more detailed benefits about Life Insurance Retirement Planning. By diversifying your investments, you can feel confident in your financial security, even in the face of market fluctuations.

- *Passive income sources*: Establishing a passive income stream that works alongside you during your working years and continues to provide additional income sources when you no longer need to work is an excellent strategy.

3. Investment Strategy:

- *Asset Allocation*: Diversify your portfolio to balance risk and return, adjusting your asset allocation as you approach and enter retirement. You can use ChatGPT, as mentioned in subchapter 5.2 above, to set up and diversify your investment portfolio.

i. One of my favorite books for asset diversification is "Multiple Streams of Income" by Robert G. Allen (#ad Scan the QR code below to get it from Amazon).

- *Risk Management*: Include a mix of growth-oriented and income-generating investments to protect against market volatility and inflation.

4. Healthcare and Insurance:

- *Health Insurance*: Plan for healthcare costs, including Medicare, supplemental insurance, and long-term care insurance.
- *HSA account for healthcare expenses*: Maximize your contribution to an HSA account (invest this fund in the S&P 500) to establish a supplement source for retirement healthcare expenses and to take advantage of triple tax benefits: tax-deductible contribution, tax-free on investment gain, tax-free withdrawal for health-qualified expenses at retirement.
- *Long-Term Care*: Consider long-term care insurance or other strategies to cover potential long-term care needs, which can be a significant financial burden in retirement. A stand-alone LTC cost will be very high. It is wise to consider adding this as a rider option in your Life Insurance IUL account to save premium costs.

5. Debt Management:

- *Debt Reduction*: Aim to reduce or eliminate high-interest debt before retirement to decrease financial pressure and increase disposable income.
- *Mortgage:* Decide whether to pay off your mortgage or carry it into retirement based on your financial situation and interest rates.

6. Tax Planning:

- *Tax-Advantaged Accounts*: Contributions to tax-deferred advantaged retirement accounts like 401(k)s and IRAs to benefit from tax deferrals and free contribution matching from your employer.
- *Tax Efficiency*: Strategize your withdrawals from different investment accounts (tax-deferred, tax-free, and taxable) to minimize tax liabilities during retirement and avoid triggering taxable income on Social Security Benefit. The important key is to ensure total withdrawals from taxable and tax-deferred accounts plus 50% of your social security plus all your earned dividends income must remain under provisional income limits ($25000 for single; $32,000 for married couples in the year 2024); that way, you will not trigger taxable income on your social security benefit. The remaining of your retirement income will come from tax-free investment accounts. It is critical to consult with your professional tax planner to optimize and balance your investment contributions between the tax-deferred, tax-free, and taxable investment accounts. I highly recommend you read or get an audible book, *"The Power of Zero"* by David McKnight (#ad Scan the QR code below to get it from Amazon). You will learn a great deal from that book about how to strategize for tax efficiency and optimize your retirement planning.

7. Estate Planning:

- *Wills and Living Trusts*: Create or update your will and consider establishing a living trust to manage your assets and protect your heirs. If you are working, sign up for a legal service plan during your employer enrollment the year you plan to set this up to take advantage of your employer subsidize for the attorney cost to set this up.
- *Beneficiary Designations:* Ensure beneficiary designations are up-to-date on retirement accounts, life insurance, and other financial accounts.
- *Power of Attorney*: Establish a durable power of attorney for financial and healthcare decisions to ensure your wishes are carried out if you become incapacitated.

8. Emergency Fund:

- *Cash Reserves*: Maintain three months of an emergency fund in a high-return savings account to cover unexpected expenses, such as medical emergencies or major home repairs, without tapping into your retirement savings.
- Utilize Life Insurance IUL cash value account as a second source of emergency funds.

9. Regular Review and Adjustment:

- *Periodic Reviews:* Regularly review and adjust your retirement plan to reflect changes in your financial situation, market conditions, and life circumstances.
- *Professional Advice:* Consider working with a financial advisor to ensure your retirement plan is comprehensive and aligned with your goals.

In closing, the journey to a secure retirement is marked by early planning, strategic use of retirement savings accounts, mindful adherence to contribution and withdrawal rules, and a well-considered estimate of retirement needs. This path, characterized by a shift in investment strategy as retirement nears, underscores the importance of foresight, discipline, and adaptability.

This closes the chapters on money matters and the awareness and skills you need to make the most of your income over the years. Next, we look at the more human side of young adulthood, physical and mental health, and the skills we can develop to stay on the horse no matter what the ride is like!

Chapter 5 Action Summary:

1. As soon as you get a job, if your employer offers a retirement 401K/403b account with free matching contributions, sign up and allocate 5%—10% of your paycheck, enough to qualify you for the maximum benefit of company matching. Select the S&P500 index as your investment fund for low risk and fee to start positioning yourself for potential long-term growth.
2. Open an emergency savings account with a major bank that offers high-interest returns and FDIC protection. Start monthly direct deposit to build a three-month reserve fund.
3. Set up a Roth IRA or Employer Roth 401K, start allocating a percentage of your paycheck to this account, and invest in the S&P 500 index. This strategy allows you to start earning

compound interest and take advantage of tax-free earnings and withdrawals during retirement.

4. Allocate 5%-10% for your active investment into stocks, bonds, real estate, or alternative investment markets.
5. Sign up for a High-Deductible Health Plan (HDHP) to qualify for setting up an HSA account. Then, start allocating a portion of your paycheck into this HSA account and invest in S&P 500 index to take advantage of triple tax advantages: tax-deductible, tax-free earning, and tax-free withdrawal for qualifying healthcare expenses.
6. Enroll in the ESPP (employee stock purchase plan) to receive a 15% discount on company stock prices.
7. Research for a Life Insurance Index Universal Life (IUL). Make an appointment to sit down with a couple of agents to discuss the advantages and disadvantages of their policy features and benefits in more detail.
8. Review the list of *essential components of retirement planning* above and make an appointment with a retirement planner to discuss and strategize your retirement planning in more detail.

MAKE A DIFFERENCE WITH YOUR REVIEW

"A single act of kindness throws out roots in all directions, and the roots spring up and make new trees."

— AMELIA EARHART

Remember when we were all stepping into Adulthood? The rollercoaster of emotions, from excitement to nervousness. It was a new adventure. Do you recall that feeling of wishing you had a guidebook tailored just for Young Adults?

The magic is in shared experiences. Let's be that special someone who has walked the path before and survived and is now willing to join forces and shine a light for all the young adults wandering, just like you once were.

Becoming an adult is a journey of adventure and challenge. Our goal is to make this guidebook, *Real-World Life Skills for Young Adults,* accessible to all young adults. Your experiences, combined with the wisdom in this book, can become a beacon.

I humbly request your help. Be the guiding star for another young adult. Most people do, in fact, judge a book by its cover (and its reviews). So, please leave a review, share your story, and let's help another first-time entering adulthood out there.

By leaving a review, your kindness means the world to me and many young adults.

Your gift takes less than 1 minute but can change a fellow young adult's life forever.

Your review could help…

...one more young adult gain the skills they need.

...one more person finds their path in life.

...one more dream come true.

To get that 'feel good' feeling, all you have to do is…

Leave a review.

Simply scan the QR code below to leave your review:

If you feel good about helping a fellow young adult, you are my kind of person. Welcome to the club.

I'm that much more excited when this book can help you achieve Real-World Life Skills faster and easier than you can imagine. You'll love the strategies I'm about to share in the coming chapters.

CHAPTER SIX

FOSTERING MENTAL HEALTH AND MANAGING STRESS

> *"Calm mind brings inner strength and self-confidence, so that's very important for good health."*
>
> — DALAI LAMA

The subtle yet profound impact of physical activity on mental health often goes unnoticed in the mix of life's daily demands and pleasures. It is a bit like the solid bass guitar line in a complex musical composition that, although not always consciously heard, fundamentally shapes the experience. This undercurrent of movement and exertion, far beyond its visible effects on physical form, plays a pivotal role in supporting mental well-being and harmonizing mind and body in a number of favorable health outcomes.

6.1 THE ROLE OF PHYSICAL ACTIVITY IN MENTAL HEALTH

Exercise and Endorphins

Physical activity initiates a cascade of biochemical processes within the brain, most notably the release of endorphins, often dubbed the body's natural painkillers. Like a pharmacological balm, these chemical compounds elevate mood and foster a sense of well-being, counterbalancing the stress and anxiety that we may experience in modern life. This complex mechanism underscores an important truth: movement begets a positive mental state—transforming exercise from a merely physical endeavor into quite a potent therapy for depression and anxiety.

Finding the Right Activity

The search for the best form of physical activity for you is like the search for the perfect pair of shoes: a highly personal endeavor where one size does *not* fit all. For some, the rhythmic solitude of a long run provides a meditative escape; while others find joy in the communal rhythm of a dance class; or others the focused strength training in a gym. The key lies in identifying activities that fit your lifestyle and fitness level and ignite the spark of joy, making the commitment to regular exercise not a *chore* but a *cherished* part of your routine.

Integrating Physical Activity into a Daily Routine Habit

Incorporating physical exercise into one's daily routine demands creativity and intention, particularly in the face of packed schedules. Strategies for integration include cycling to work—replacing the passive inertia of the commute with the active engagement of muscles and mind; or opting for the stairs over the elevator. Even more simply, scheduling walks during lunch or coffee breaks can break the passive cycle of desk-bound work, proving that incorporating exercise need not be disruptive to be effective. One of effective methods to incorporate your exercise into your daily routine is forge it into your habit.

Understanding habits

At the core of habit formation lies a simple yet powerful neurological loop comprised of three key elements:

- Cue
- Routine
- Reward

Once initiated, this loop spins an automatic web, embedding behaviors so deeply within our psyche that they become reflexive responses to specific triggers.

- The cue acts as a catalyst, a particular signal that initiates the habit loop.
- The routine is the behavior, the action taken in response to the cue.
- The reward is the most critical component. It is the benefit derived from the behavior. It reinforces the loop and ensures its repetition.

This triad loop, operating in the shadows of our consciousness, lays the foundation for habits that serve (or hinder) our aspirations.

The psychological processes underpinning habit formation are rooted in the brain's relentless quest for efficiency. The brain always tries to conserve cognitive resources by automating routine actions, relegating these tasks to the basal ganglia, a region associated with developing emotions, patterns, and memories. This delegation frees the prefrontal cortex, the brain's executive command center, for more complex tasks, showcasing the brain's remarkable ability for optimization.

Creating new habits

The germination of new habits, particularly those aligned with positive life changes, necessitates a deliberate strategy, a conscious effort to forge paths less traveled by the mind. This transformative journey begins with identifying a clear, attainable goal to guide the construction of the habit loop:

- **Cue:** It is paramount to pinpoint an effective cue. This cue must be specific and consistently present, capable of triggering the desired routine without ambiguity.
- **Routine:** The action we wish to embed into our lives must be precisely delineated, ensuring it is practical and feasible within our daily routines.

- **Reward:** Selecting a reward that genuinely works for you, offering a sense of satisfaction or pleasure, ensures the reinforcement of the habit loop. This reward solidifies the connection between the cue and the routine, embedding the new habit within our neural pathways.

Over time, as this loop is repeated, the behavior transitions from a conscious effort to an automatic action, a courageous ally in pursuing personal growth!

Below is my personal method of forging the Habit Loop principle to my daily 20-minute morning exercise.

- **Cue (The Trigger)**: This is the WHY. I question myself why I can establish the habit of brushing my teeth every night and every morning so quickly. The triggers are fear of toothache, bad breath, and the desire to have healthy teeth. I apply the same WHY / triggers to forge my morning exercise into a daily habit to avoid fatigue and unproductiveness, and I want to build strong muscles and vibrant health. I consider my body and mind to be just like the phone I depend on daily. My physical body is like the phone's hardware, and my mind is like the phone's software. Just like a phone must be recharged daily to function, my body also requires daily energy recharging to function healthily and productively.
- **Routine:** This is the HOW and WHAT. I build and optimize my morning exercise routine through YouTube tips for yoga, tai chi, qigong, cardio exercise, and breathing techniques. I start with five to six simple moves, three minutes each, that bring me joy, peace, and satisfaction. The best way is to start with small, short 15–20 minutes daily to reinforce consistency over intensity, and gradually increase when the habit has been established. *The key is joy and consistency*.
- **Reward:** This is the satisfaction payoff. Excellent health, a great body, and a great look will help you feel full of energy, more productive, and more confident. All these satisfactions will help release a surge of neurochemicals, such as dopamine,

which is associated with pleasure and joy, which reinforces the brain's association between trigger and routine, establishing the good feedback of the habit loop.

Habit stacking

The construction of complex routines from more straightforward habits, a strategy known as habit stacking, offers a systematic approach to comprehensive lifestyle change. This technique involves the sequential integration of new habits onto existing ones, creating a cascade of positive behaviors initiated by a single cue. The beauty of habit stacking is in its simplicity and ability to bring about significant change through small, incremental steps. By anchoring each new habit to a preexisting one, we build a range of routines that collectively sculpt our lives characterized by continual improvement and deliberate living.

To initiate habit stacking, one begins with a basic habit, a behavior already firmly embedded in our daily routine, and links a *new* habit to completing that foundational habit. This linkage creates a chain of actions, each triggering the next. As this chain lengthens, the complexity of the routine grows, yet its execution remains streamlined, powered by the pure momentum of habit.

This method not only simplifies the integration of new behaviors but also fortifies the structure upon which our daily lives are built, ensuring that each action, no matter how small, is a step towards realizing our highest aspirations.

An example of habit stacking is linking a quick morning shower, then a healthy morning smoothie drink after 20 minutes of daily exercise. These three—exercise, shower, and healthy smoothie drink—have the same trigger: desire for good health, and even act as triggers for one another, reinforcing an even more vital link of habit loops.

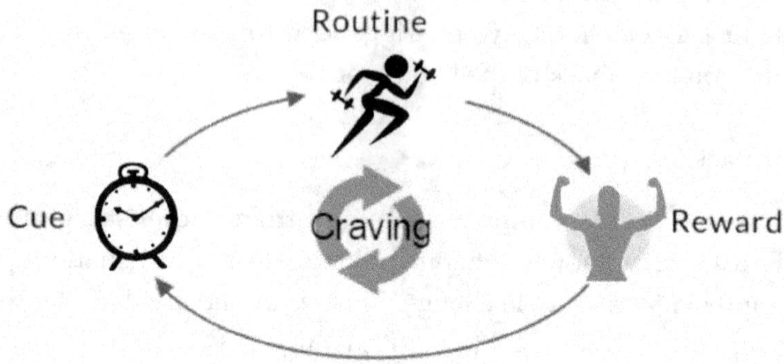

THE HABIT LOOP

Reference [33]

In this dynamic interplay of movement and mental health, physical activity emerges not as a panacea but as a vital component of a broader strategy for well-being, a self-care action that, when done with intention and understanding, contributes to the richness of our mental and physical lives. As we experience the joys and challenges of life, the deliberate integration of exercise into our daily routines stands as a testament to our commitment to holistic health, mental resilience and clarity.

Action checklist:

1. Establish your WHY. Identify your main objective and benefits that help trigger and urge you to exercise.
2. Start building your 20-minute daily routine by searching YouTube, Instagram, or TikTok to establish your own five or six exercise movements: cardio, burn fat, build strength, or tai chi. Do whatever makes you feel good!.
3. Enroll in a group exercise or fitness dance group (if you enjoy group exercise)

6.2 UNDERSTANDING STRESS: CAUSES AND EFFECTS

Identifying Stressors

In the highly stimulated lives of young adults today, stress often becomes an unwelcome companion, lurking in the shadows of ambitious career goals and the intricacies of personal relationships. This invisible adversary, capable of infiltrating every aspect of our lives , needs a vigilant approach to identification and management.

Recognizing the multiple sources of stress—a crucial first step in this endeavor—demands a keen awareness of one's internal reactions to external pressures. With expectations and deadlines, career ambitions frequently sow seeds of anxiety, as do the dynamics of ever-evolving personal relationships, which can oscillate between sources of joy and then wellsprings of tension. Financial concerns may further compound this lineup of stressors. Young adults are facing such a lineup daily.

Physical and Emotional Impact and Stress Response

The toll exerted by this stress on the body and mind is profound and pervasive. Physiologically, it triggers a cascade of responses designed for survival, yet when perpetually activated, this system strains the body, leading to symptoms such as headaches, fatigue, and sleep disturbances. Emotionally, the impact is equally significant, with stress manifesting through anxiety, irritability, and depression. Early recognition of these symptoms is important, signaling the need for intervention before the storm of stress gains further momentum.

The natural stress response is at the heart of the body's arsenal against threat, a primordial mechanism that galvanizes the individual into action through the "fight or flight" response. This biological alarm system, sophisticated in its simplicity, prepares the body to confront or flee from perceived threats. Understanding this response illuminates the reasons behind stress's physical and emotional symptoms, underscoring the importance of strategies that either mitigate the perceived danger or modulate the body's reaction. Within this understanding, the power lies in transforming your relationship with stress—from victimhood to informed management.

Long-Term Consequences

The shadow cast by stress extends beyond immediate symptoms, heralding potential long-term health consequences if left unaddressed. The chronic activation of the stress response can precipitate a decline in physical health, ushering in a host of issues such as hypertension, heart disease, and a compromised immune system. Similarly, mental health can become scarred by prolonged exposure to stress, with an increased risk of developing anxiety disorders, depression, and a pervasive sense of burnout. This stark reality accentuates the critical nature of early and effective intervention. Stress management is an essential tool for enhancing quality of life and a preventative measure against a range of health concerns.

The journey through young adulthood is punctuated by challenges that test one's resilience and adaptability. Recognizing stressors, understanding their impact on the body and mind, and being aware of the potential for long-term health consequences inform good, effective stress management strategies, that we look at now.

6.3 TECHNIQUES FOR STRESS REDUCTION

Mindfulness and Meditation

In an era where the din of daily obligations may often drown out the harmony of life's simpler pleasures, mindfulness and meditation emerge as tranquil practices. These ancient yet timeless traditions invite exploration into the present moment, advocating a gentle yet profound attentiveness to the *here and now*. Mindfulness, the art of maintaining a moment-by-moment awareness of our thoughts, feelings, bodily sensations, and surrounding environment, offers us a more vivid experience of life— without the overlay of judgment or preconception. Meditation, its close relative, provides a structured approach to cultivating this awareness through techniques that may include focused attention on breath, mantra repetition, or guided visualization—each path leading toward deep relaxation and heightened awareness.

If you are taking the initial steps into mindfulness and meditation, the terrain may seem daunting, strewn with misconceptions about the need for empty minds or prolonged sessions of stillness. The reality, however, is far more accessible. Challenging reactions such as restlessness, skepticism, and impatience are common companions on this journey. Overcoming these hurdles begins with acknowledging their presence, treating them not as obstacles—but as opportunities for deeper engagement with the practice. If you start with brief sessions, embrace the imperfections, and experiment with various forms of meditation, that will demystify the process, revealing a practice that is not about the *cessation* of thought—but the *observation* of it, without attachment or judgment.

I recommend checking out *MindValley.com*, an online platform with many meditation apps and self-learning personal development programs. https://www.mindvalley.com/

Time Management Strategies

Living up to the constant stream of responsibilities and deadlines demands resilience, and strategic insight into managing our most finite resource: time.

Effective time management is less about the rigid adherence to schedules and more about the mindful allocation of energy, so that priorities dictate the flow of our days, rather than the whims of circumstance. Apply techniques such as the Eisenhower Box for tasks priority assessment method, which categorizes all daily tasks into Urgent vs. Important. Set top priority and time to tackle tasks that are both urgent & important, plan and schedule tasks that are important but not urgent, delegate or delay tasks that are urgent but not important (e.g., reply to group or friends' emails or text), and eliminate tasks that are neither important nor urgent. Other strategies, such as reducing the friction of task switching, and a realistic to-do list can help streamline the accomplishment of daily goals. At its core, effective time management aligns actions with priorities, carving out space not just for the urgent things, but for the meaningful—thereby reducing stress by elevating control and intention in your daily endeavors.

Reference [43] for Eisenhower Matrix for tasks priority

Healthy Social Interactions

We humans—inherently social beings—draw strength and solace from connections. Positive social interactions, characterized by empathy, understanding, and mutual respect, can soothe life's stresses as well as give joy and inspiration. In fostering relationships that support and uplift, individuals find reservoirs of resilience and buffers against the ups and downs of life. Nurturing these connections involves active listening, expressing appreciation, sharing experiences, and creating interpersonal relationships rich with the potential for mutual growth and support. Conversely, discernment is needed to distance yourself from toxic or draining interactions. This is equally vital, protecting mental well-being and preserving energy for those relationships that truly nourish.

In drawing this chapter to a close, the techniques for stress reduction include mindfulness and meditation to illuminate the beauty of the present, task priority management strategies to instill a sense of control and purpose, and healthy social interactions to provide support and joy. These techniques, diverse in their approaches yet unified in their purpose, offer a blueprint for living with a reduced burden of stress, leading toward a future where well-being and fulfillment are not just aspirational *goals* but lived *realities*.

As we turn our gaze ahead, my advice to you continues into the realms of essential life skills, where the principles of self-care and stress management support the everyday tasks and decisions that shape our adult lives.

Chapter 6 Action Summary:

1. Establish a 20-minute daily exercise habit and incorporate it into your daily routine to improve mental health.
2. Download apps to practice mindfulness and meditation to reduce stresses
3. Download time management or task prioritize apps to optimize and effectively manage your time to reduce stress.
4. Search for social interactions that align with your interests, nurture your connections, share experiences, and create personal relationships rich with potential for mutual growth and support.

CHAPTER SEVEN
ESSENTIAL SKILLS FOR EVERYDAY LIVING

> *"The secret of getting ahead is getting started."*
>
> — MARK TWAIN

In the adult world, where responsibilities loom large and time seems to remain in perpetually short supply, the art of meal preparation is an important part of self-reliance. It's an arena where the alchemy of nutrition meets the pragmatism of budgeting, all choreographed alongside a ticking clock. For those in the early stages of independent living, the kitchen often represents the final frontier of domestic mastery—a place where the chaos of separate ingredients can transform into the lovely harmony of a nourishing meal!

7.1 NUTRITIONAL FUNDAMENTAL: HEALTHY, QUICK, AND BUDGET-FRIENDLY RECIPES

Nutritional Basics

Understanding the fundamentals of nutrition is like decoding a map before venturing out on uncharted terrain. It's about recognizing that each meal is an opportunity to fuel the body with the macronutrients—proteins, fats, and carbohydrates—and micronutrients—vitamins and minerals—that it requires to thrive. This awareness informs choices, guiding the selection of whole grains over refined ones, favoring lean proteins, and embracing a rainbow of fruits and vegetables to ensure a good range of nutrients.

Essential nutrients are substances that the human body requires for proper functioning, growth, development, and overall good health. These nutrients must be obtained through our diet since the body cannot produce them in sufficient quantities. The essential nutrients can be broadly categorized into six main groups:

1. **Carbohydrates**: Carbohydrates are the body's primary source of energy. They are broken down into glucose, which fuels cellular activities and provides energy for physical activity. Good sources of carbohydrates include fruits, vegetables, whole grains, legumes, and starchy foods like potatoes and rice.
2. **Proteins**: Proteins are essential for building and repairing tissues and synthesizing enzymes, hormones, and antibodies. They are made up of amino acids, some of which are essential because the body cannot produce them independently. Protein-rich foods include meat, poultry, fish, eggs, dairy products, legumes, nuts, and seeds.
3. **Fats**: Fats are a concentrated energy source and play a vital role in cell structure, hormone production, and nutrient absorption. They also provide insulation and protection for organs. Healthy fats, such as monounsaturated and polyunsaturated fats found in olive oil, avocados, nuts, and fatty fish, should be included in the diet. In contrast, saturated and trans fats should be limited.
4. **Vitamins:** Vitamins are organic compounds essential for various metabolic processes, immune function, and overall health. They are classified into two groups: water-soluble vitamins (such as vitamin C and B-group vitamins) and fat-soluble vitamins (such as vitamins A, D, E, and K). Each

vitamin has specific functions and can be obtained from a balanced diet that includes a variety of fruits, vegetables, whole grains, and animal products.

5. **Minerals**: Minerals are inorganic substances essential for maintaining fluid balance, nerve function, muscle contraction, and bone health, among other functions. They include macrominerals such as calcium, magnesium, phosphorus, sodium, and potassium, and trace minerals like iron, zinc, copper, iodine, selenium, and chromium. Minerals are found in various foods, including dairy products, leafy greens, nuts, seeds, seafood, and fortified foods.
6. **Water**: Water is essential for life and is involved in virtually every bodily function, including digestion, circulation, temperature regulation, and waste removal. It is vital to stay hydrated by drinking adequate water throughout the day and obtaining water from hydrating foods like fruits and vegetables.

A balanced diet that includes a variety of nutrient-rich foods from all food groups is essential for meeting the body's nutritional needs and maintaining optimal health. Additionally, individual nutrient requirements may vary based on age, sex, activity level, and health status.

Meal Planning and Grocery Shopping

Awareness of this fundamental nutritional knowledge will simplify your weekly meal planning and help you eat more healthy and balanced diets. There are many benefits to pre-planning your weekly meals. Just one to two hours on Sunday to plan out weekly meals for the week ahead will free you up from daily stress about what to eat and cook. It also helps to gear you toward a more healthy and balanced diet. You will have more time to relax and enjoy doing other things you love after work.

Weekly meal planning also helps streamline your grocery shopping trips into more strategic, targeted trips and prevents impulse buys. In addition, creating a detailed list segmented by store sections will help save time and money, minimize food waste, and ensure every purchase has a purpose in the week's culinary story!

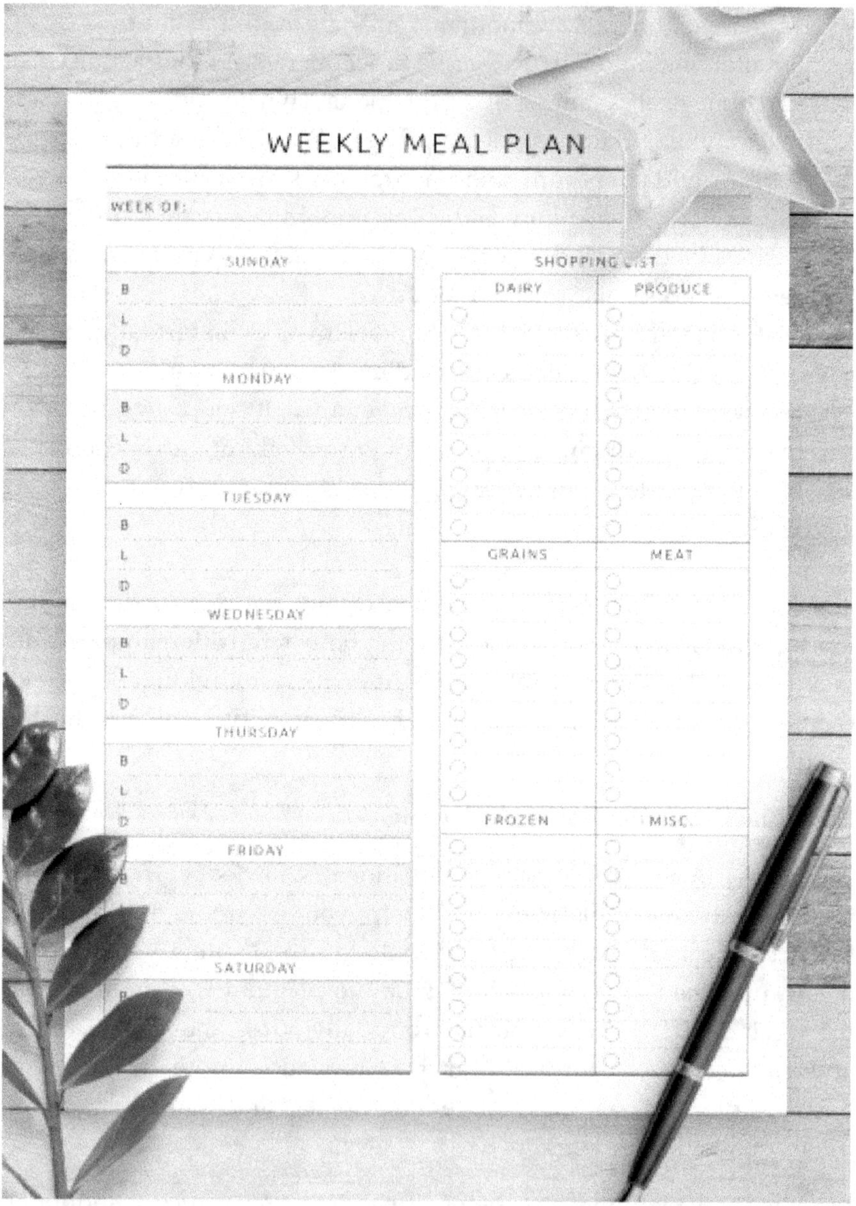

Reference [35]

Quick and Easy Recipes

For many busy individuals, preparing quick and easy daily meals is essential for maintaining a healthy lifestyle without sacrificing too much time or going to a lot of effort. Fortunately, numerous simple yet delicious recipes can be whipped up quickly using common ingredients found in most grocery stores.

Below are a couple of examples of simple, quick and healthy recipes:

- Hearty vegetable stir-fry involves tossing a variety of colorful vegetables, such as bell peppers, broccoli, carrots, and snap peas, with boiled eggs, pre-cooked chicken, or beef in a hot skillet with a flavorful sauce made from soy sauce, ginger, garlic, and a splash of sesame oil. Serve it over cooked rice or noodles for a nutritious and satisfying meal.
- Another go-to option is a classic pasta dish like spaghetti aglio e olio, which translates to spaghetti with garlic and oil. This dish requires just a handful of ingredients, including spaghetti, garlic, olive oil, red pepper flakes, and parsley. Cook the pasta until al dente, then sauté minced garlic and red pepper flakes in olive oil until fragrant. Toss the cooked pasta in the garlic-infused oil, sprinkle with chopped parsley, and voila! You have a flavorful pasta dish that's ready to enjoy in minutes!
- YouTube search "quick healthy meal recipes" for more quick tips.

For those seeking more inspiration, countless online resources and cookbooks are dedicated to quick and easy meal recipes. Some popular sources include 30-Minute Meals by Rachael Ray, Quick Recipes by New York Times Cooking, and websites like Allrecipes.com and Food Network's Quick and Easy Recipes section. These sources offer many ideas and tips for creating delicious meals in no time, making it easier than ever to eat well—even on your busiest days.

Food Safety and Storage

Navigating food safety and storage is critical, ensuring that the effort invested in meal preparation yields dividends throughout the week. It involves understanding the temperature danger zone, recognizing the shelf life of prepared foods, and employing proper storage techniques to prevent spoilage and foodborne illnesses. For instance, cooling cooked dishes rapidly before refrigeration and storing them in clear, airtight containers extends their freshness and makes for an inviting visual reminder of ready-to-eat options.

In the domain of essentials life skills, mastery of meal prep stands as proof of one's ability to nurture oneself with intention and efficiency. It reflects a balance between the nutritional needs that sustain us, the budgets that constrain us, and the schedules that demand our agility. Through the lens of meal preparation, we encounter the tangible expression of self-care—a ritual that feeds the body *and* the soul.

7.2 BASIC HOME/CAR ROUTINE MAINTENANCE AND REPAIRS

A DIY GUIDE

Routine Home Inspection Checklist and Maintenance Schedule

For those stepping into the wonderful world of homeownership or independent living, the upkeep of your dwelling is a responsibility that, while at times may seem daunting, is essential for ensuring the longevity and safety of your living space. A carefully crafted checklist and calendar reminder will help you to make a periodic assessment of your home's condition, identifying potential issues before they might escalate into costly repairs. This checklist encompasses various areas:

1. Exterior home Inspection:

- Check the condition of the roof, looking for missing shingles, signs of damage, or leaks.

- Inspect gutters and downspouts for debris, clogs, and proper drainage away from the foundation.
- Examine siding, brickwork, or stucco for cracks, deterioration, or signs of moisture intrusion.
- Inspect windows and doors for air leaks, damaged seals, or signs of rot.
- Check the condition of the foundation for cracks, settling, or water damage.

2. Interior home Inspection:

- Test smoke detectors and carbon monoxide detectors, and replace batteries if needed.
- Inspect electrical outlets, switches, and fixtures for proper functioning and signs of wear.
- Check for plumbing leaks under sinks, around toilets, and behind appliances.
- Test faucets and toilets for leaks, proper water pressure, and drainage.
- Inspect ceilings, walls, and floors for water stains, cracks, or signs of structural issues.
- Check HVAC systems (heating, ventilation, and air conditioning) for proper operation and replace central air filters every six months to ensure good air circulation and fresh air for your home. Write down the date/year on the new filter for future reference.

3. Safety Checks:

- Test fire extinguishers and ensure they still work and are accessible, or better, purchase on Amazon a maintenance-free fire extinguisher blanket for quick and simple use
- Personal safety kit backpack for nature disasters (shoes, jacket, portable first aid kit, flashlight, nutrition bars)
- Emergency choking rescue device. (can be purchased on Amazon)

- Inspect stairways, railings, and banisters for stability and safety.

4. Appliance and Equipment Inspection:

- Inspect kitchen appliances for proper functioning, leaks, or signs of wear.
- Test the water heater's operation and check for leaks or corrosion. Flush the tank annually to remove sediment and debris.
- Clean dryer vents and exhaust ducts to prevent fire hazards.
- Clean the washing machine's drain pump filter regularly. To locate the filter, refer to the user manual on YouTube.
- Clean the washing machine's drum by running a cleaning cycle with hot water and detergent or a mixture of vinegar and baking soda.

Routine Car Inspection Checklist and Maintenance Schedule:

Regular car maintenance checkups will help minimize costly repairs, prevent unexpected breakdowns on the road, and keep your car running optimally and lasting longer.

Below are a few simple and essential maintenance activities:

1. **Oil Changes**: Set calendar reminders or utilize a trip B odometer to keep track of mileage for oil changes. Synthetic oil covers more mileage (7K miles to 10K miles) than conventional oil (5K miles to 7K miles). Synthetic oil has a more uniform molecular structure and thus performs better under higher and extreme temperature ranges than conventional oil.
2. **Tire Rotation and Alignment**: Rotating your tires helps ensure even wear and extends the tire's lifespan. Alignment checks and adjustments help maintain proper tire alignment, improving handling and reducing wear. Maintain the recommended PSI pressure for safety, gas-saving, and overall good driving experience. The manufacturer's recommended

PSI tire pressure label is usually located on the side of the driver's door.

3. **Brake Inspections**: Regular brake inspections are crucial for safety. It includes checking brake pads, rotors, calipers, and brake fluid levels for signs of wear or leaks.
4. **Fluid Checks and Top-Ups**: Regularly check fluid levels, including coolant, transmission fluid, brake fluid, power steering fluid, and windshield washer fluid, and top them up as needed.
5. **Air Filter Replacement**: Replace your engine air filter and cabin air filter as your vehicle's manufacturer recommends to maintain engine performance and improve air quality inside the car.
6. **Battery Maintenance**: Inspect your car battery regularly for signs of corrosion, leaks, or low voltage. Clean terminals and ensure a secure connection to prevent starting issues.
7. **Spark Plug Replacement**: To maintain fuel efficiency and engine performance, replace spark plugs at the recommended intervals. Search YouTube for tips and steps.
8. **Check Engine Light Diagnosis**: Address any warning lights on your dashboard promptly by diagnosing the issue to prevent potential damage or further problems.
9. **Wiper Blade Replacement**: Replace worn wiper blades to ensure visibility during inclement weather conditions.
10. **Suspension and Steering Maintenance**: Inspect suspension components, such as shocks, struts, and ball joints, for signs of wear or damage to help improve ride quality and handling.
11. **Cooling System Maintenance**: To prevent overheating and engine damage, maintain your vehicle's cooling system by flushing and replacing coolant according to manufacturer recommendations.

Car Emergency Tool Kit:

1. Manufacturer emergency tool kits (a spare tire and jack) are usually in the car's trunk.

2. Prepare a jumper cable or portable battery jumping device
3. Portable power air pump/compressor for emergency flat tire
4. Emergency window/windshield glass breaker & seatbelt cutter tool
5. Duct tape to temporarily fix hoses, belts, or other parts
6. Glove, blanket, flashlight

Each tool serves a specific purpose yet collectively represents your readiness to tackle a range of repairs and projects. This arsenal, though compact, is mighty, equipping the homeowner and auto owner with the means to confront challenges with assurance and skill.

DIY household projects:

Empowering oneself to make minor home repairs independently is a cornerstone of self-sufficiency. It transforms reliance on external assistance instead into personal growth and skill development opportunities. The benefit of having these basic skills is self-control and confidence when any household issue occurs, in addition to time *and* financial savings.

In today's Information Age, everything is at your fingertips. YouTube videos with DIY step-by-step tips can help you fix many simple household repairs, such as a clogged drain, leaky faucet, or hole in the wall, and all major household appliances (washing/dryer machine, refrigerator). Always go to YouTube and look up an issue you are facing for quick repair tips before calling a service contractor. It will save you a *lot* of time and money.

Learning how to fix things yourself will give you a sense of self-control, wonderful self-confidence, and a constantly growing mindset.

7.3 PERSONAL SAFETY: AWARENESS AND SELF-DEFENSE BASICS

Self-Awareness of Surrounding:

In our modern existence, where the threads of safety and danger can interweave subtly, the skill of situational awareness stands out as crucial—a proactive stance empowering individuals to anticipate and, if necessary, neutralize threats in their early stages. This heightened alertness, far from any paranoia that clouds the enjoyment of life's offerings, is a balanced vigilance—an almost subconscious scanning of environments for anomalies that might indicate potential risk.

Self-Defense Basics:

Transitioning from the macrocosm of situational awareness to the microcosm of physical autonomy, basic self-defense techniques are essential knowledge, equipping individuals with the means to protect their bodily integrity in situations where avoidance and de-escalation have faltered. Learning techniques for breaking free from various holds is essential. These moves can be learned from various online social platforms (YouTube, Instagram, TikTok) and practiced with your close friends—or through certified professionals who can provide physical training *and* the psychological preparedness to act decisively in moments of peril.

Successful living in modern society requires from us the amalgamation of situational awareness, self-defense skills, and the strategic formulation of a safety plan, constituting a multifaceted personal protection approach. This dynamic and adaptable framework empowers individuals to respond to threats with informed action, and live with a sense of security that fosters *freedom* rather than constraint.

7.4 DIGITAL DETOX: BALANCING ONLINE AND OFFLINE LIFE

Recognizing digital overload

In an era where the digital world infiltrates almost every aspect of our daily existence, digital overload has becomes an inevitable side effect for many of us. This saturation of screens and notifications, relentless and unyielding, often leads to a state where the boundary between user and device blurs, with profound implications for mental and physical well-being. Identifying the symptoms of this overload is the initial step towards reclaiming autonomy over the use of technology.

These symptoms manifest as a persistent feeling of being overwhelmed, difficulty concentrating, disrupted sleep patterns due to blue light exposure, and a noticeable decline in face-to-face interactions. Recognizing these signs is like reading the early warning signals that the body and mind send out, indicating a need for recalibration and a return to healthier equilibrium.

Setting boundaries

Establishing healthy boundaries with technology is not a *retreat* from the digital world but a strategic renegotiation of its place in our lives. It involves setting specific times for checking emails and social media, preventing these activities from fragmenting daily attention. Designating tech-free zones, especially in bedrooms and dining areas, fosters environments conducive to rest and genuine connection with others. For those tethered to devices by the demands of work or study, employing apps that monitor and limit usage can provide an objective lens through which to view and adjust behavior. This conscious digital engagement, far from being a draconian measure, is a liberating reassertion of control, allowing for a healthier interaction with technology—acknowledging its benefits while mitigating its drawbacks.

Benefits of unplugging

The benefits of regular periods of disconnection, or "digital detoxes", extend beyond alleviating overload symptoms. Whether they last a few hours each day or are observed as tech-free weekends, these periods reacquaint individuals with the pleasures and possibilities of the offline world. Unplugging reopens the doors to hobbies and interests that may have been sidelined, rekindles the joy of immersive reading without the lure of hyperlinks, and revitalizes the art of conversation, free from the "ping" of notifications. Moreover, the space created by stepping away from screens often leads to a surge in creativity and productivity, as the mind, unshackled by the constant demand for attention, finds new pathways to explore and problems to solve. This re-engagement with the actual, physical world, with its tactile experiences and unmediated interactions, enriches life in a manner that virtual reality strives to emulate—but can never fully replicate.

Enjoy your digital portion of life by recognizing signs of overload, strategically setting boundaries, rediscovering offline joys, and cultivating purposeful engagement. Though personal and unique to each individual, this journey shares a common destination, connecting us to the world in enriching, empowering, and, ultimately, *human* ways.

7.5 PRIVACY AND SECURITY: SAFEGUARDING YOUR DIGITAL LIFE

In an age where the boundaries between the real and the virtual blur, the sanctity of personal privacy and security assumes paramount importance. For all its many conveniences, this digital era casts a shadow of vulnerability over individual privacy, making safeguarding one's digital existence prudent and necessary. You need an understanding of the basics of online privacy, while adhering to security best practices; know the nuances of data sharing and consent; and recognize the meticulous curation of one's digital footprint.

Online Privacy Basics

At the core of digital privacy lies the imperative to protect personal information from unauthorized access, which demands vigilance and strategic insight. Though seemingly subtle, the distinction between personal and sensitive information is crucial. The latter encompasses data that, if compromised, could lead to identity theft or financial loss. Encryption becomes a stalwart ally in this battle, encoding data so that only those with the key can decipher it, transforming sensitive information into indecipherable code during its journey across the internet. Regularly reviewing the privacy policies of websites and apps before engagement informs you how their data is used and empowers you to proceed or seek alternatives.

Security Best Practices

The cornerstone of digital security is creating and maintaining strong, unique passwords for each online account, a practice that significantly reduces the risk of unauthorized access. Using password managers facilitates this task, storing and generating complex passwords that defy the attempts of cyber-intruders. Two-factor authentication adds an additional layer of defense, requiring a second form of verification beyond the password, a hurdle that few hackers can surmount. In email, the discernment to identify phishing attempts is vital. Phishing is fraudulent communications aiming to elicit sensitive information. These emails often masquerade as legitimate requests from reputable sources, yet subtle clues, such as generic greetings or misspelled URLs, betray their nefarious intentions.

Digital Footprint Management

Every online activity, from social media posts to online purchases, contributes to one's digital footprint, an indelible mark etched into the memory of the internet. Managing this trail demands a proactive approach, regularly searching your own name to gauge the scope of your online visibility and taking steps to remove or secure information that increases vulnerability. Adjusting social media settings to restrict the audience of posts and being judicious in the information shared online curtails the spread of personal data. Furthermore, deactivating or deleting old accounts without current purpose eradicates dormant data points that cyber-predators could exploit.

In the ever-evolving digital landscape, where innovation and risk are inextricably linked, vigilance in safeguarding your online life is a crucial skill. It encompasses a range of practices, from the basic understanding of privacy principles to the careful management of your digital footprint. Following this advice, with your constant alertness and application of adaptive strategies, means you will navigate the digital realm confidently and securely, preserving your privacy and protecting your personal information against the endless tide of cybercrime.

7.6 MISINFORMATION: CRITICAL THINKING IN THE INFORMATION AGE

Discerning the truth from the spurious in our online era is an exercise in cognitive agility. The omnipresence of misinformation, cloaked in the guise of authenticity, demands another vigilant, analytical stance. Facing this challenge, while formidable, is not impossible; it necessitates honing critical thinking skills and a sharpening of the intellect to slice through the Gordian knot of half-truths and falsehoods that are pervasive in the digital landscape.

Developing critical thinking skills

Cultivating critical thinking skills and ability will see you rise above the tide of misinformation. It is a process that begins with acknowledging one's biases, the invisible lenses through which we view the world, which can distort our perception and interpretation of information. From this basis of self-awareness, developing these skills involves questioning assumptions, seeking diverse perspectives, and engaging in reflective thought. It is a disciplined approach to thinking, where questions wielded with precision can dismantle the flimsy facades of unfounded claims, revealing reason (or the absence thereof) beneath.

Fact-checking and verification

Armed with critical thinking, you will be well-equipped to embark on fact-checking and verification, a careful venture that underpins the integrity of information. This endeavor leverages a toolkit of resources, from established fact-checking organizations to primary source materials, each serving as the light of truth in the fog of misinformation. Techniques in this process mirror the rigor of scientific inquiry, where claims are tested against evidence, sources are scrutinized for their reliability, and conclusions are drawn based on the weight of factual corroboration.

Next up, we look at a much more personal subject to learn and enjoy (and sometimes despair!) in young adult lives: relationships!

Reference [37-39] for additional home repair resources.

Chapter 7 Action Summary:

1. *Prepare your own home inspection checklist and set reminder for annual inspection*
2. *Prepare your own car maintenant checklist and set reminder for routine maintenant*
3. *Get an emergency tools kits for your car*
4. *Sign up for self-defense class or search youtube and bookmark self-defense techniques to escape from dangerous situations and practice with friends and buddy.*
5. *Establish a routine for Digital detox to get out more to nature or more outdoor exercise and activities*

CHAPTER EIGHT
NAVIGATING RELATIONSHIPS AND COMMUNICATION

> *"The quality of your life is the quality of your relationships."*
>
> — TONY ROBBINS

In the rich experiences known as human interaction, the subtle yet quite profound act of listening is a thread that binds the fabric of relationships, transforming mere exchanges into deep, meaningful connections. The art of active listening, often overshadowed by the urge to express yourself, holds the power to unlock depths of understanding and empathy. At its essence, active listening transcends the sensory process of hearing words, and ventures into the realm of *feeling* the speaker´s emotions and intentions—a bridge built not of hard, cold stone but of warmth, attentiveness and compassion.

8.1 THE POWER OF ACTIVE LISTENING

Active listening involves a constellation of skills: a focused attention that silences the clamor of one's thoughts to truly hear another person speak, the patience to allow silence to breathe and speak, and the empathy to step into another's shoes, viewing the world through their lens. This dynamic process transforms listeners into mirrors, reflecting not just the words spoken but the emotions and *unspoken* truths hidden within. The significance of this transformation lies not in the mere exchange of information but in the deepening of bonds, the building of trust, and the nurturing of an environment where vulnerability is met with understanding, rather than judgment.

Practicing Active Listening

Imagine a scenario at a local coffee shop where two friends meet. Amidst the hum of background chatter and the clinking of cups, one shares the turmoil of a recent loss. Here, active listening manifests in the other friend leaning in, the nodding of the head, the absence of interruptions, and the murmuring of words that convey empathy—not advice. This scene, simple yet profound, encapsulates the essence of active listening. Beyond this, exercises to hone this skill can be integrated seamlessly into daily life: from repeating in one's own words what was just heard, to validate the speaker's message, to asking open-ended questions that invite elaboration, peeling back the layers of surface dialogue to reveal the deeper core of what is indeed being communicated.

Barriers to Effective Communication

Distractions loom as formidable barriers in this quest for connectivity. The omnipresent screens that vie for our attention, the internal rehearsals of what to say next, and the judgments that cloud perception are a few of the veils that obscure proper understanding. Recognizing these barriers is the first step towards dismantling them—a conscious effort to clear the path for genuine exchange.

Reference[40] for additional resources related to active listening & Effective Communication

Impact on Relationships

The transformation inspired by active listening in relationships is much like the alchemy of turning base metals into gold. It cultivates an atmosphere where individuals feel heard and valued, where conversations become channels for deeper understanding, rather than battlegrounds for asserting opinions! Through this lens, conflicts become opportunities for growth, misunderstandings are stepping stones to greater clarity, and relationships (hopefully!) evolve into sanctuaries of mutual respect and appreciation.

Active listening is a practice enriched by intentionality and a willingness to engage with the complexities and subtleties of human emotion and thought. This chapter invites readers to transform their approach to communication, fostering relationships that are not only resilient, but deeply rewarding.

8.2 CONFLICT RESOLUTION STRATEGIES

Conflict emerges not as an anomaly but as an inherent rhythm in human relationships, a testament to the diversity of thoughts, feelings, and desires that characterize our interactions. Far from signaling the demise of a relationship, conflict, when approached with intention and skill, can serve as a crucible for growth and understanding. It beckons us to sail the choppy waters of disagreement with a compass calibrated not toward victory—but toward mutual understanding and resolution.

Understanding the Nature of Conflict

At the heart of the conflict lies *differences,* whether in opinion, need, or expectation. This divergence, inherent to the human condition, need not be a harbinger of division but a portal to deeper connection. Recognizing conflict as a natural aspect of relationships demystifies its presence, stripping away the fear and resistance that often accompanies it. Embracing conflict as an *opportunity* rather than a threat allows engagement with divergent perspectives as a fertile ground for innovation, empathy, and strengthening bonds. Within this framework, conflict moves from being held in a battleground to a meeting place—where differing views can coexist, through respectful dialogue, and be learned from.

Steps for Resolving Conflict

Navigating conflict resolution demands a sequential approach, a choreography of steps that guide from discord to harmony. The initiation of resolving conflict game plan begins with:

1. Identify and acknowledge existing of a conflict between involved parties.
2. Prepare for a resolution, plan a neutral and private setting, and ensure all parties are calm and willing to discuss the issue.
3. Allow each person to express their views without interruption or judgment. Understanding that human brains are wired differently for each individual, thus perceive things differently.
4. Focus on identifying the root cause of the underlying issues and finding a resolution, separating human emotion from the problem.
5. The choice of language is a game-changer, and the use of 'I' statements offers a personal perspective on the issue (e.g., 'I feel... '), diffusing defensiveness and paving the way for empathy.
6. Active listening, a critical component in conflict resolution, ensures that each party feels heard and respected, fostering a sense of validation and understanding.
7. Consider involving a neutral third party to mediate if the conflict is complex and highly emotional.

From this foundation of mutual understanding, identifying underlying needs and concerns allows for distilling conflict to its essence, revealing common ground previously obscured by the fog of disagreement. It is upon this common ground that solutions can be co-created, in a process of collaborative brainstorming that seeks not compromise, (where each party relinquishes something), but a synergistic resolution that meets the needs and desires of all involved. This inclusive and often challenging step requires patience, creativity, and a steadfast commitment to the relationship over the rather selfish ego.

It is always easier said than done. One of the most challenging obstacles is detaching emotions from the problem. We are an emotional species; thus, naturally, it is very easy to fall into the trap of getting emotionally frustrated over why other people couldn't see what I was seeing; it was so obvious! We usually don't understand the intricacy of human brains, which are neurologically and emotionally wired differently from person to person when looking at things. Getting emotionally frustrated will cause all communication channels between involved parties to shut down or shield off. From there on, no matter how logically it makes sense to you or how much energy you put into trying to find solutions for the problem, your effort won't get through or be recognized. As a result, it will keep getting you deeper into a circle of emotional frustration. However, by recognizing the trigger of the emotional trap and understanding that people's brains are neurologically and emotionally wired differently, you will be one step ahead, avoid falling into the emotional trap, and equip yourself to be better and more successful when facing the inevitable life conflicts.

The Role of Apologies and Forgiveness

Integral to resolving conflict is the exchange of apologies and the granting of forgiveness, acts of humility and grace. An apology, genuine and unencumbered by justification, acknowledges the hurt or harm inflicted, intentionally or not, serving as a bridge to reconciliation. It signals a willingness to take responsibility, providing an element of trust and respect in any relationship.

Forgiveness, in turn, is the act of releasing resentment, a deliberate decision to let go of grievances and the desire for retribution. It neither negates accountability nor condones the action, but frees both parties from the shackles of past hurts, enabling movement forward. It is in the magical mix of apologies and forgiveness that healing and growth occurs, transforming the scars of conflict into badges of resilience.

Preventing Escalation

The prevention of an escalation of conflict lies in the early detection of warning signs and the implementation of de-escalation tactics. Recognizing the heat of emotions as the signal to pause—breathe—and step back from the precipice of escalation forms the first line of defense. Within this pause lies the opportunity to employ calming techniques, revisit the intentions behind the engagement, and choose a path *away from further* discord.

Strategies such as agreeing to take a time-out, rephrasing statements to ensure clarity and non-confrontation, and maintaining an open posture and tone, will all contribute to de-escalating tensions. Mindful engagement is a practice that focuses on resolution and understanding, guiding actions and words toward cooling tempers and preventing harm.

After the Resolution

The aftermath of conflict resolution, marked by a return to calm and a sense of closure, offers fertile ground for deepening relationships. It is a time for reflection, assessing the conflict resolution process, and acknowledging lessons learned. This reflective practice, undertaken individually and collectively, serves to fortify the relationship against future conflicts, embedding resilience and adaptability into its DNA.

Rebuilding trust, an essential component of post-conflict recovery, unfolds gradually through consistent actions and reaffirming your commitment to the relationship. It is bolstered by open communication, the continuous practice of active listening, and the mutual respect that underpins healthy interactions. Strengthening the relationship post-conflict involves reaffirming affection and commitment, and implementing strategies gleaned from the resolution process, supporting a stronger, more understanding connection moving forward.

8.3 SETTING BOUNDARIES IN RELATIONSHIPS

Boundaries serve as the invisible architecture upon which the building of personal well-being and relational health is constructed. Much like the meticulously drawn lines on an architect's blueprint, they delineate the spaces wherein individuality breathes, and relationships flourish, safeguarding the sanctity of personal values, emotional needs, and physical spaces. To erect boundaries is not an act of division but a declaration of respect and self-worth, a necessary distinction that fosters autonomy while nurturing interdependence. Within any relationship, well-defined boundaries ensure that interactions don´t develop into power struggles but into dialogues of mutual respect and understanding.

Boundary setting is rooted in the profound act of self-reflection. In this solemn introspection, personal values are not merely identified but are honored as the guiding stars of one's existence. This reflective process demands unflinching honesty, a willingness to acknowledge your needs, limits, and expectations, and recognize that these deserve protection. It is an inward journey that maps out the terrain of your comfort levels, identifying those core aspects of self that must remain inviolate for your essence to remain unblemished.

Thus, the act of delineating personal boundaries becomes a testament to self-awareness—a tangible expression of the understanding that in order for one to thrive, certain principles must remain sacrosanct, untouched by the external pressures or demands of others.

Communicating these boundaries to others is an art that requires not just courage but finesse in articulation, ensuring that the message conveyed is not one of alienation but of self-respect and mutual regard. The essence of this communication lies in clarity and assertiveness, in the ability to communicate your needs and limits without ambiguity or apology. This dialogue, often preemptive, sets the tone for future interactions, establishing a framework within which relationships can develop without infringing upon personal sanctity. It is an exercise in assertiveness that, far from breeding conflict, lays foundations for deeper understanding and respect.

Strategies for effective boundary communication encompass a range of practices, from the pragmatic—such as the use of "I" statements that focus on the speaker's feelings and needs rather than assigning blame —to the strategic, like choosing an appropriate moment for discussion, one devoid of tension and conducive to receptivity.

Examples of setting boundaries in various relationships:

1. Emotional Boundaries

- Example 1: "I need to have time alone to process my feelings when I am upset."
- Example 2: "I appreciate your advice, but I would prefer to make my own decisions. If I need advice, I will ask for it."

2. Physical Boundaries

- Example 1: "I am not comfortable with hugging; a handshake is fine."
- Example 2: "Please knock before entering my room."

3. Time Boundaries

- Example 1: "I need to leave by 9 PM, so we can plan to meet earlier."
- Example 2: "I can only dedicate two hours to help with this project."

4. Intellectual Boundaries

- Example 1: "I respect your opinion, but I have a different viewpoint on this matter."
- Example 2: "Let's agree to disagree on this topic."

5. Material Boundaries

- Example 1: "I can lend you my car, but please return it with a full tank of gas."
- Example 2: "I prefer not to lend my books; they are very important to me."

6. Digital Boundaries

- Example 1: "Please do not share my photos on social media without asking."
- Example 2: "I need to turn off my phone after 10 PM to relax before bed."

Yet, even the most clearly communicated boundaries can be breached through inadvertent or willful disregard. Handling such violations is a delicate endeavor that tests the resilience of one's commitment to self-respect. The initial reaction, often a blend of disappointment and anger, is a natural response to the transgression of personal space. However, the subsequent action must be measured—guided by the principle that the breach offers an opportunity for *reaffirmation* rather than retaliation. Addressing the violation directly with the party involved, reiterating the boundary with renewed clarity, and expressing the impact of the breach on one's emotional state are all steps that facilitate the resolution of the immediate issue and the prevention of future infractions.

In instances where violations persist, implementing consequences—actions that reinforce the seriousness with which one regards their boundaries—becomes necessary. When predetermined and communicated in advance, these consequences underscore the non-negotiable nature of one's limits, deterring further breaches.

In the complex life of human relationships, the setting, communication, and defense of personal boundaries are all critical skills that safeguard your emotional and physical space, allowing for the flourishing of individuality within the broader context of interdependence. These boundaries demand not just recognition but respect—both from oneself and from others. Through the careful process of identifying these non-negotiable aspects of your existence, articulating them with clarity and confidence, and addressing any violations with firmness and dignity, you will manage your various relationships with grace and self-assurance.

Reference[41] for additional resources relate to setting boundaries in relationships.

8.4 BUILDING YOUR SUPPORT NETWORK: FRIENDS, MENTORS, AND MORE

Importance of a support network

A multifaceted support network emerges as a pivotal anchor in our lives, offering guidance, inspiration, and solace. This network, a constellation of relationships that spans the spectrum from friends and family, to mentors and professional allies, serves as both a bulwark against isolation and a catalyst for ongoing personal and professional development.

Finding mentors

The search for mentors who have navigated the waters we find ourselves sailing in is a testament to the very human yearning for guidance and wisdom. By sharing their journey, these seasoned voyagers illuminate uncertain paths, their insights a lighthouse for those of us in uncharted territories. Identifying such mentors necessitates discerning alignment in values, aspirations, and challenges, acknowledging that the mentorship journey is one of mutual respect and learning. Cultivating these relationships requires proactive engagement, an openness to feedback, and a commitment to action—transforming receiving advice into stepping stones toward realizing one's potential. The dynamics of mentorship, rooted in authenticity and trust, inevitably evolve, changing the mentor-mentee relationship into a partnership of lifelong learning and growth.

Expanding your social circle

Expanding one's social circle, a venture that enriches your life with diverse lines of connection, demands an active foray into new environments and communities. This expansion, while daunting, thrives on the willingness to step beyond the comfort of familiar shores to engage with new ideas, cultures, and perspectives. The initiation of conversations, participation in community events, and even joining clubs or groups that echo one's interests and values all serve as channels for forming new friendships. These new connections, nurtured through shared experiences and a consistent investment of time and energy, gradually coalesce into *meaningful* relationships, enriching one's life with a kaleidoscope of insights, experiences, and support.

In contrast, the maintenance and deepening of existing relationships require an intentional cultivation, a mindful effort to sustain and enrich the bonds forged over time. This endeavor, far from a passive expectation of mutual engagement, calls for a deliberate investment of time, a conscious effort to communicate, and a genuine interest in the evolving lives of those within one's circle. Regular check-ins, sharing experiences, and celebrating milestones and achievements reinforce these relationships, affirming their significance and fostering a mutual growth that will stand the tests of time.

Quality over quantity

In nurturing a robust support network, quality over quantity is a good guiding principle, emphasizing the value of deep, meaningful connections over many superficial acquaintances. This focus on quality, taking a discerning approach to relationship-building, champions the depth of connection that nurtures the soul, supports growth, and withstands the ups and downs of life. It acknowledges that the strength of one's support network is not measured by its size, but by the richness of understanding, empathy, and encouragement that it provides. In this context, each relationship is a treasure, a unique blend of shared history, mutual respect, and collective aspiration.

From the seeking of mentors who light the path with their wisdom, to the expansion of one's social circle with individuals who share one's passions and values, each step in this process contributes to the creation of a network that is both a shield against adversity and a wellspring of inspiration. This network, characterized by the quality of its connections and the diversity of its composition, represents the interconnectedness of our human experience.

8.5 NAVIGATING ROMANTIC RELATIONSHIPS: COMMUNICATION,TRUST, AND MUTUAL RESPECT

In romantic relationships, the bedrock upon which enduring partnerships are built lies in the interplay between open, honest dialogue and the mutual trust and respect underpinning it. Each exchange, steeped in genuine interest and concern for your partner, builds a bridge over which love travels back and forth, drawing two souls closer in their shared journey. The essence of this communication transcends the mere exchange of words; it embodies the sharing of dreams, fears, and the minutiae of daily life, creating a world of shared experiences that binds hearts together. When nurtured in an atmosphere of respect, such dialogue allows for the flourishing of individuality within the union, fostering a relationship where each partner feels valued, heard, and cherished.

Foundations of healthy relationships

A romantic relationship involves several critical components that contribute to its health, longevity, and satisfaction for both partners. Below are some of the most crucial elements:

1. Communication

Effective communication is foundational in a romantic relationship. This includes being open about feelings, thoughts, and expectations, as well as actively listening to each other. Good communication helps prevent misunderstandings and resolves conflicts constructively.

- **Example:** Regularly checking in with each other and discussing both everyday occurrences and deeper emotional experiences.

2. Trust

Trust is essential for a secure and stable relationship. It involves being reliable, honest, and maintaining fidelity. Trust allows partners to feel safe and confident in their relationship.

- **Example:** Being transparent about one's actions and intentions and keeping promises.

3. Respect

Mutual respect means valuing each other's individuality, opinions, and boundaries. Respecting differences and supporting each other's growth fosters a healthy dynamic.

- **Example:** Listening to each other without judgment and appreciating each other's perspectives.

4. Emotional Support

Providing and receiving emotional support helps partners cope with stress, challenges, and personal growth. This includes being empathetic, understanding, and encouraging.

- **Example:** Being there for each other during difficult times and celebrating successes together.

5. Intimacy

Intimacy, both emotional and physical, strengthens the bond between partners. It involves sharing personal experiences, being vulnerable, and maintaining physical affection.

- **Example:** Regularly spending quality time together and maintaining a physical connection.

6. Commitment

Commitment involves dedicating time, effort, and energy to the relationship and planning a future together. It signifies a long-term intention to maintain and grow the relationship.

- **Example:** Setting joint goals and working together to achieve them.

7. Compatibility

Compatibility in values, interests, and life goals is essential for long-term harmony. While differences can be enriching, having common ground in key areas supports a stable relationship.

- **Example:** Sharing similar views on major life decisions such as family planning, career goals, and lifestyle choices.

8. Conflict Resolution

The ability to handle disagreements and conflicts in a healthy manner is crucial. This includes using constructive communication, compromising, and finding solutions that satisfy both partners.

- **Example:** Addressing issues calmly and seeking to understand the root cause rather than blaming each other.

9. Shared Activities and Interests

Engaging in activities together and having shared interests helps maintain a strong connection and enjoy each other's company.

- **Example:** Participating in hobbies, traveling, or taking on new projects as a team.

10. Individual Growth

Encouraging each other's personal development and maintaining a sense of individuality within the relationship is important for both partners to feel fulfilled.

- **Example:** Supporting each other's career aspirations, education, or personal hobbies.

Reference [42-43] reference sources

As we turn the page, we carry forward the lessons learned in the experience of romantic relationships, a reminder that the strength of our connections, whether romantic or otherwise, lies in our ability to communicate with honesty, trust, mutual respect, and to embrace differences with empathy and understanding. These principles, universal in their application, guide us not only in intimate love—but in all manners of human connection, illuminating the path for relationships that are not just enduring, but genuinely enriching.

Romance is a magical part of life, where we find our loving natures fully engaged. You will feel vulnerable at times, but have the courage of your heart and choose your partner wisely. There is great spiritual growth inspired by close relationships. Sex is to be enjoyed, but remember to use protection if you are not wishing to start a family!

Now we step away from romance and come to the chapter on enhancing productivity and time management. If you manage your time well, you can spend more time with your romantic partner!

Chapter 8 Action Summary:

1. Practice active listening and effective communication.
2. Review vital steps in resolving conflict.
3. Apply boundary-setting strategy for your various day-to-day relationships.
4. Aware of essential components of social and romantic relationships.

CHAPTER NINE
CULTIVATING A MINDSET FOR GROWTH

> *"Success is not to be pursued; it is to be attracted by the person you become."*
>
> — JIM ROHN

In our early adulthood and throughout our lives, a silent tension exists within the confines of our minds—tension between growth and stagnation, between the allure of comfort and the challenge of expansion. This internal dynamic shapes not just the contours of our life stories but the very essence of our being, determining the heights we reach and the depths we explore. At the heart of this struggle lies the concept of mindset—a potent force that wields the power to anchor us to the familiar, or propel us into endless and unknown possibilities.

9.1 GROWTH VS. FIXED MINDSET

In our world teeming with diversity, where unique trials and triumphs mark each person´s path, the distinction between a growth mindset and a fixed mindset emerges as a critical juncture, determining the direction of one's personal and professional evolution. A growth mindset, characterized by the inherent belief in the malleability of abilities and intelligence, serves those seeking to transcend their own perceived limitations. It champions the idea that personal growth is not just a possibility but a *certainty* with effort, perseverance, and a willingness to embrace challenges. In contrast, a fixed mindset, rooted in the belief that abilities are static and unchangeable, casts a shadow over our potential, stifling the drive for learning and viewing setbacks as insurmountable barriers.

Therefore, the important benefits of adopting a growth mindset cannot be overstated. It infuses life with resilience, transforming obstacles into stepping stones and failure into a springboard for new discoveries. This mindset nurtures an openness to learning, fueling the relentless pursuit of knowledge and skills that broaden horizons and deepen understanding. It fosters a resilience that buffers against any negativity in life, ensuring that each setback is met with renewed vigor.

Identifying Fixed Mindset Triggers

Navigating the transition from a fixed to a growth mindset begins with identifying triggers—those moments when the siren song of comfort tempts us to view effort as futile, and challenges as threats. These triggers often lurk in the shadows of our failures, the sting of criticism, or the daunting face of the unknown. Recognizing such triggers requires some introspection, a reflective pause in the midst of busy life to discern the moments when our self-limiting beliefs about ourselves hinder our progress.

Consider, for instance, learning a new language, a task that beckons with the promise of new experiences, but also introduces the potential peril of embarrassment and failure. The initial excitement often gives way to frustration in the face of complex grammar and unfamiliar sounds. In these moments of discomfort, the fixed mindset whispers of inherent linguistic incompetence, urging retreat to the safety of the known. Recognizing this trigger, however, allows for a conscious choice—a decision to persist, to embrace the discomfort as a sign of growth, and to view each stumble not as evidence of incapacity—but as a step towards mastery.

Transitioning to a Growth Mindset

The path towards a growth mindset is paved with intentionality and nurtured by habits reinforcing the firm belief in personal evolution. It involves a deliberate reorientation of perspective, viewing life as an environment rich with opportunities for learning and self-discovery. This transition is facilitated by practices that embed the principles of growth into the fabric of daily life.

Assessing your mindset quiz here:

https://blog.mindsetworks.com/what-s-my-mindset

Reference[52]

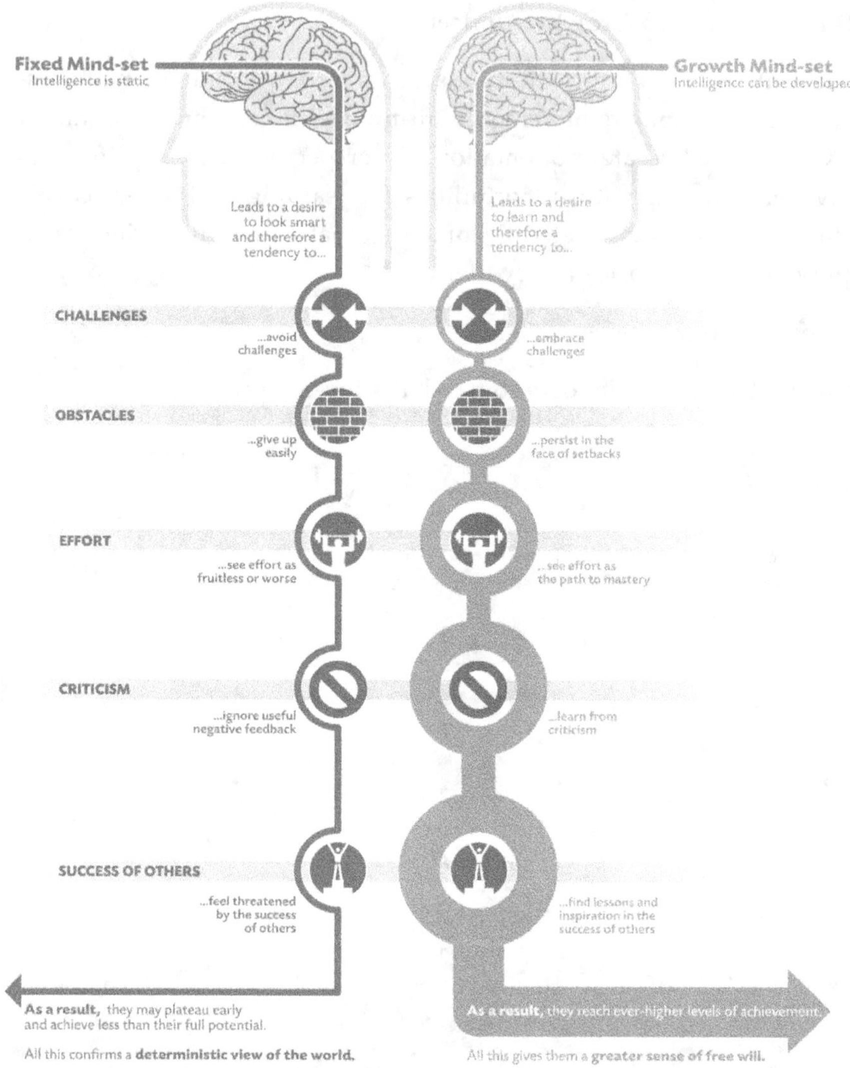

One practical step in this transition involves reframing challenges as opportunities. When faced with a daunting task, instead of recoiling at the prospect of failure, ask, "What can I learn from this experience?" This simple question shifts focus from the *outcome* to the *growth process*, encouraging a mindset that values progress over (impossible) perfection.

Another strategy involves embracing feedback as a gift rather than a grievance. Constructive criticism, when you have a growth mindset, becomes a roadmap for improvement, highlighting areas where effort and learning can lead to advancement.

Engagement in continuous learning is the product of a growth mindset. It signals a commitment to perpetual personal evolution, acknowledging mastery is not a destination, but a journey marked by continual exploration and adaptation.

Cultivating a growth mindset is not a passive activity but an active pursuit, a conscious choice to view life as an endless series of lessons and opportunities for expansion. It demands resilience in the face of setbacks, courage to venture beyond your comfort zone, and an unwavering belief in the potential for transformation.

In embracing this mindset, we unlock the doors to personal and professional fulfillment, moving toward a future limited only by the boundaries of our imagination.

9.2 THE ROLE OF FAILURE AND SELF-IMPROVEMENT IN GROWTH

Reframing Failure

Moments that first appear to be failures are, upon closer inspection, rich with growth potential. Shifting the perspective on these instances from definitive endpoints to integral steps in the learning process moves the emotional response from defeat to opportunity. It is a subtle yet profound adjustment in viewpoint, recognizing that each stumble and fall adds a layer of depth and resilience to our character. This reevaluation of failure as a necessary precursor to success is not just an attempt at consolation—it is a reorientation toward the reality that growth is often fertilized by the seeds of our most challenging experiences.

Analyzing Failures Constructively

Distilling wisdom from disappointment requires an analytical approach. This analysis goes beyond surface-level scrutiny, delving into the decisions, actions, and inactions that steered your course toward an undesired result. Employing reflective journaling or structured debriefs with friends or mentors allows for a comprehensive examination of the failure, ensuring that the insights gained are acknowledged and internalized. The objective is to acknowledge the misstep while highlighting the adaptive strategies and insights gained, thus paving a way forward that is positively informed by experience rather than touched by regret.

Embracing Risk-Taking

Cultivating a mindset that welcomes taking calculated risks as a natural component of the learning process is key in the journey toward self-improvement and achievement. This acceptance of risk-taking as a worthwhile endeavor shifts the focus from the potential for failure to the potential for discovery and innovation. It encourages stepping out of comfort zones with the knowledge that, regardless of the outcome, the experience will contribute to a richer understanding and an expanded repertoire of skills. By viewing risk this way, the fear associated with potential failure diminishes, and is replaced by an anticipation of the learning opportunities that await.

Receiving Feedback Positively

Personal and professional growth requires an openness to feedback and a willingness to absorb and reflect upon the perspectives of others. Receiving feedback, particularly when it highlights areas for improvement, requires a fortitude that views such exchanges as *gifts* rather than grievances. Strategies to facilitate this positive reception include active listening, suspending immediate defensive reactions, and practicing gratitude for the insights provided.

Using Feedback for Improvement

The ultimate goal of soliciting feedback is to harness those insights for personal and professional development. This involves the deliberate process of sifting through the feedback received, identifying actionable items, and integrating these into a plan for improvement. It demands a balance between receptivity to external perspectives and the discernment to align the feedback with one's own values and goals. Adopting this structured approach to incorporating feedback makes each piece of advice a gift contributing to continuous growth and refinement.

The interplay between failure, risk, and feedback supports the essence of growth—a dynamic process that challenges, shapes, and ultimately propels us forward.

Reference[53] for additional resources.

Reflection and Growth

In the quiet moments of our bustling lives, the act of turning inward, of holding a mirror to the self, is a sacred ritual. This introspection, removed from the clamor of daily existence, serves as a channel for genuine self-awareness and growth. The practice of regular self-reflection, therefore, is not merely an exercise in thought, but the cornerstone of personal development, a deliberate pause to assess where we stand in relation to where we wish to be. It demands honesty, courage, and a willingness to confront both our shining achievements and the shadows cast by our inevitable shortcomings. Through structured reflection, guided by a journal or quiet contemplation, we chart our progress, celebrate our victories, and acknowledge areas ripe for improvement. This quiet ritual, found in the rhythm of our lives, ensures that growth remains not an abstract wish but a tangible, ongoing pursuit.

9.3 READING AND LEARNING: EXPANDING YOUR KNOWLEDGE BASE

The pursuit of knowledge, a quest as ancient as humanity itself, takes place across our lives, providing enlightenment and shades of understanding. This quest, driven by our insatiable curiosity, finds its roots in the fertile ground of reading and learning—activities that support personal and professional growth. In this context, learning transcends its traditional age-related limits, becoming a lifelong endeavor that continually reshapes our perspective and refines our understanding of the world and our place within it.

The emphasis on lifelong learning emerges not merely as an educational philosophy, but as a vital strategy for navigating the complexities of the modern world. This approach to learning recognizes that the acquisition of knowledge and the development of skills are not confined to the formative years of schooling, but extend throughout the entirety of one's life. The impact of this continuous engagement with learning is profound, fostering adaptability, enhancing creativity, and bolstering our capacity to address the challenges and opportunities that life presents.

In the realm of reading, the selection of books becomes an important decision, a deliberate choice that steers the direction of our intellectual voyage. The ocean of literature, vast and deep, offers millions of options, each promising to carry the reader on new journeys. However, the selection of books that significantly contribute to personal growth demands your discernment—an ability to sift through the multitude to find those rare gems that offer not just information, but *transformation*. These are the books that challenge our thinking, offer new perspectives, and inspire us to question and explore. They are the catalysts for change, pushing us beyond the comfort of established paradigms and into the realm of new possibilities. The advice for choosing such books leans on relevance and diversity—the relevance to your goals and interests, ensuring engagement and application; and diversity in subjects, which exposes you to a broad spectrum of ideas and disciplines, enriching your cognitive landscape.

Active reading further enhances the usefulness and impact of this literary exploration. More than just the passive consumption of words, active reading (quite like active listening, that we have already looked at) is an engagement with the text, a dialogue between the reader and the author that demands concentration, reflection, and interrogation. Techniques such as annotating the margins, summarizing chapters, and questioning the author's assumptions and arguments transform reading from a solitary activity into an interactive learning process.

This engagement ensures that the information enters and resonates within your mind, fostering deeper comprehension and long-lasting retention. Active reading, thus, becomes a tool not just for learning—but for thinking critically, and creatively.

The digital realm also offers diversity, through online courses, podcasts, and workshops. Each medium offers unique advantages, catering to different learning styles and preferences. Online courses, with their structured curriculum and interactive components, provide a comprehensive learning experience, allowing for the exploration of subjects in depth. Podcasts, conversational and accessible, offer insights and perspectives on a wide range of topics, making learning a part of your everyday routine. Workshops, emphasizing practical application and peer interaction, foster a hands-on approach to learning, cementing knowledge through experience. This eclectic mix of learning sources ensures a rich and varied educational diet, stimulating intellectual growth and fostering a culture of continuous learning.

9.4 CULTIVATING HAPPINESS: PRACTICES FOR WELL-BEING

In all the many experiences in human life, happiness often emerges as a coveted, perhaps elusive thread, its colors vibrant, yet seemingly just beyond reach. This quest for happiness, while universal, unfolds uniquely within each life, suggesting that its essence can be distilled into a skill—a cultivated art that blossoms through intentional practice. Happiness reveals itself through life experiences, achieving goals for personal growth, and a deep sense of purpose and meaning. Unraveling this in your own life requires exploring the core components that form the bedrock of happiness, guiding us toward practices that will elevate our well-being.

Happiness from Life Experiences

Happiness through life experiences calls for an immersion into the present, a conscious decision to engage fully with the world around us. It is in the laughter shared with friends, the awe of a breathtaking view, and the thrill of a new adventure that happiness finds its expression. These moments, rich with vitality, underscore the importance of presence, of savoring the *now* rather than being entangled in the *what-ifs* of the past and future.

To harness this aspect of happiness, one might create a 'Bucket List of Joy,' a compilation of experiences, both grand and simple, that ignite a spark of joy in you. This list acts not as a tally, but as a reminder to blend happiness into the mix of your daily life, encouraging engagement with the world in a manner that nourishes the soul.

Happiness from goals achievement

Pursuing happiness through goal achievement holds the promise of fulfillment, showcasing the resilience and determination of the human spirit. This dimension of happiness thrives on the progression of setting and reaching milestones that resonate with our deepest aspirations. However, the key lies not in the *culmination* but in the *journey*, the growth and learning accompanying each step toward our goals. A 'Growth Tracker,' a tool for setting, monitoring, and reflecting on personal goals, facilitates this process. It allows you to articulate objectives, break them into actionable steps, and offers a space for reflection on the lessons learned along the way. This practice transforms goal achievement from a race to a rhythm, a harmonious balance between striving and becoming.

Happiness from purpose and meaning

Happiness through finding purpose and meaning emerges as a compass that directs our actions, infusing our endeavors with depth and significance. This dimension of happiness transcends the singular person, connecting us to something greater through community, creativity, or contribution. Attaining happiness through purpose and meaning involves introspection, a turning inward to unearth the values and passions that drive us. A 'Purpose Map,' a reflective guide, aids in this discovery, prompting questions that delve into our most profound motivations and aspirations. By charting a course that aligns with these inner truths, we can cultivate a happiness that is both enduring and enriching, rooted in the knowledge that our lives reflect our most authentic selves.

Happiness from practicing Gratitude

Gratitude, a practice as ancient as it is powerful, is also a cornerstone in the architecture of happiness. The simple yet profound act of acknowledging the good in our lives shifts our focus from scarcity to abundance—from what is lacking to what is plentiful. Maintaining a 'Gratitude Journal,' a daily record of moments, people, and experiences for which we are thankful, nourishes an attitude of appreciation that permeates our perception, affecting our interaction with the world. This habit of mind, nurtured over time, becomes the lens through which the beauty and bounty of life are magnified, enhancing our overall well-being.

Happiness from acts of kindness

Happiness, through acts of kindness—both spontaneous and deliberate—weave threads of connection and compassion into the fabric of our communities, bolstering not only the happiness of others, but also our own. The principle that *happiness grows through giving* is evident in small gestures and grand acts, each creating ripples in the pond of human experience. To incorporate this practice into the rhythm of life, one might consider a 'Kindness Calendar,' a schedule of intentional acts of kindness. It could range from words of encouragement to acts of service, each fostering a sense of fulfillment and connection. This practice underscores the truth that in lifting others up, we elevate ourselves, finding happiness in the well-being of our fellow travelers.

Happiness through appreciation the majestic beauty of nature

The connection with nature, an elemental, often overlooked source of happiness, calls us back to our roots, a world governed by natural rhythms and cycles, rather than clocks and calendars. Immersing ourselves in the natural world, whether through a walk in the park, a day by the sea, or a hike through the mountains, reconnects us with the earth and its boundless beauty. This reconnection, a return to the simplicity and majesty of nature, calms the mind and rejuvenates the spirit, offering a respite from the clamor of modern life. To integrate this connection into our lives, a 'Nature Engagement Plan' might detail regular outdoor activities, encouraging a routine that includes the natural world as a source of peace, beauty, and happiness.

These practices—rooted in experiences, growth, purpose, gratitude, kindness, and nature—serve as guideposts in navigating the path toward happiness. They illuminate the journey toward well-being and remind us that happiness—far from being a distant dream—is a *skill* to be cultivated, a garden to be tended with intention and care.

9.5 BUILDING A LEGACY: WHAT WILL YOUR IMPACT BE?

In the quiet theater of our hopes, where dreams flicker like shadows cast by a fire's glow, the notion of legacy commands a profound presence. It represents our desire to carve out a space in the annals of time —to leave behind a mark that speaks of our journey, values, and the lives we've touched. This desire, inherently human, pushes us to consider the path we tread and the footprints we leave behind.

Defining Your Legacy

At the core of this introspection lies the challenge of defining the legacy we would like to bequeath. This intensely personal yet universally significant task beckons us to sift through the layers of our lives to distill the essence of our aspirations into a coherent vision. It compels us to ask, "What is the impact I wish to have?" and "How do I want to be remembered?" This quest for definition is not the pursuit of vanity, but a reflection of our deepest yearnings to contribute to the world in a manner that reflects our most authentic selves. It is a process that demands honesty, courage, and a willingness to confront our achievements *and* shortcomings, weaving them into a narrative that captures the essence of *who we are* and *what we stand for*.

Impact Through Work

For many, the arena of professional endeavor emerges as a potent conduit for legacy building. Our careers, from the mundane to the monumental, offer a unique platform for influence, a stage upon which we can enact change, inspire innovation, and mentor the next generation. However, the impact of our professional lives transcends the boundaries of personal achievement, touching the lives of colleagues, clients, and communities. Our professional legacy is forged in our dedication to excellence, our commitment to ethical practice, and perhaps our drive to push beyond the known limits of our fields. This legacy, crafted through years of toil and triumph, shines a light for those who follow, a guidepost signaling paths to success and fulfillment.

Community Involvement

Beyond our professional lives, community involvement offers a fertile ground for legacy cultivation. Whether through volunteerism, activism, or philanthropy, engagement with our communities echoes our values and priorities, broadcasting them through actions that speak louder than words. This involvement, characterized by a selfless dedication to the welfare of others, sows the seeds of a legacy rooted in compassion, service, and social responsibility. It reflects our understanding that true fulfillment derives not from what we accumulate—but from what we contribute. It is a principle that elevates our existence from the solitary to the communal.

Personal Values and Legacy

The most enduring legacies are those inextricably linked with our values, those core principles that guide our decisions, shape our actions, and define our character. Aligning our legacy with these values ensures that our impact resonates with authenticity, reflecting a life lived in harmony with our most profound convictions. This alignment requires a deliberate effort to embody our values in every facet of our lives, to act as living proof of the ideals we hold dear. It is a process of continuous reflection and adjustment, a commitment to live not just for the moment, but for the imprint we leave on the hearts and minds of those we touch.

In crafting our legacies, we engage in acts of creation that extend beyond the boundaries of our own lives, reaching into the future to touch generations yet unborn. It is a declaration of our values, contributions, and aspirations reflected through the lives we lead and the choices we make. As we navigate through the complexities of existence, let us do so with an eye toward the legacy we wish to leave, understanding that each moment presents an opportunity to contribute to a narrative that will outlive us.

Chapter 9 Action Summary:

1. Take a mindset quiz assessment._https://blog.mindsetworks.com/what-s-my-mindset
2. Latch on to the path of a growth mindset by embracing changes and challenges, viewing setbacks as opportunities for learning and self-discovery. Perceive feedback and criticism as gifts and motives for self-development and improvement.
3. Set a goal of reading more personal growth books to expand your knowledge. Practice active reading by annotating what you read, summarizing chapters, and questioning the author's assumptions and arguments. Commit to life-long learning by making learning a part of your everyday routine and through various sources, such as online courses, podcasts, or workshops.
4. Cultivate happiness for health and well-being through setting goals and achieving them, through purpose and meaning, through life experiences and exploring nature's wonder of the natural world, through practicing gratitude and acts of kindness.
5. Accumulate your experiences and personal values, build your legacy, and share them with communities.

CONCLUSION

"Real-World Life Skills for Young Adults" not only emphasizes the importance of equipping oneself with essential skills for life, but also illuminates the *transformative* potential that lies within each key competency. Throughout this book, we have delved into various aspects of personal and professional development, highlighting the practical value they bring to one's life, and the profound changes they can bring about.

We began by highlighting the fundamental significance of life skills, elucidating how they serve as indispensable tools for navigating the multifaceted challenges of adulthood. From financial acumen to emotional resilience, from career planning to interpersonal communication—each skill plays a pivotal role in shaping one's journey toward success and fulfillment.

Reflecting on the key points covered in each section, we have explored strategies and insights to empower readers to take charge of their own lives. Whether devising a budget, setting career goals, practicing self-care, or nurturing meaningful human connections, every chapter has offered practical guidance for fostering personal growth and empowerment.

Indeed, empowerment through knowledge and action lies at the heart of this endeavor. By arming yourself with newfound knowledge and skills, you are equipped and empowered to approach life's challenges with confidence and determination. You have the power to make informed decisions, overcome obstacles, and seize opportunities for growth and advancement.

As you embark on your journey of self-discovery and development, I encourage you to reflect on the wisdom imparted within these pages. I hope you do not merely absorb information passively but actively engage with it, integrating lessons learned into your daily life. I urge you to set tangible goals, devise actionable plans, and take deliberate steps toward realizing your aspirations.

Inevitably, the pathway to mastering life skills is fraught with challenges and setbacks. Yet, it is precisely through perseverance and resilience that actual growth occurs. We remind readers that setbacks are not failures—but rather invaluable opportunities for learning and growth, and should be embraced as such. In times of doubt or difficulty, may you draw strength from within, seek support from loved ones, and press onward with an unwavering determination.

As this book draws to a close, I extend a final call to action to you all, our dear readers: Let this be the beginning of your journey toward personal and professional excellence! Beyond these pages lie boundless opportunities for further learning and growth. I urge you to seek out workshops, join online communities, and explore additional resources dedicated to the ongoing advancement of your life skills.

Finally, remember that the power to shape your destiny lies squarely in your hands. Embrace this journey wholeheartedly, for the path to success is paved with dedication, resilience, and a commitment to lifelong learning.

Farewell, dear reader, and may your pursuit of happiness and excellence be as enriching as it is rewarding!

KEEPING THE REAL-WORK LIFE SKILLS CONTINUES PAYING FORWARD TO ALL YOUNG ADULTS

Now you have everything you need to master Real-World Life Skills; it's time to pass on your newfound knowledge and show other readers where they can find the same help.

By leaving your review of this book on Amazon, you're not just sharing your thoughts, you're contributing to a community of young adults who are passionate about *"Real-World Life Skills for Young Adults"*. Your review is invaluable in guiding others to the information they're looking for.

Thank you for your single act of kindness. You are a crucial part of keeping the spirit of *"Real-World Life Skills for Young Adults"* alive when we pass on our knowledge – and your kindness is helping us to do just that.

Scan the QR code below to leave your review:

REFERENCES SOURCES:

1. McGill University. (n.d.). How to identify your strengths and weaknesses. McGill Career Planning Service (CAPS). Retrieved from https://www.mcgill.ca/caps/students/explore/self-assessment
2. Ameer, M. (2022, August 17). How to identify your personal strengths and weaknesses LinkedIn. Retrieved from https://www.linkedin.com/pulse/how-identify-your-personal-strengths-weaknesses-muslim-ameer
3. The Muse. (n.d.). 43 best resume tips for landing a job in 2023. The Muse. Retrieved from https://www.themuse.com/advice/43-resume-tips-that-will-help-you-get-hired
4. Hired. (2023, January 12). How to write an ATS-friendly resume: 6 tips to reach recruiters. Hired. Retrieved from https://hired.com/blog/candidates/write-ats-friendly-resume-2023-6-tips-reach-recruiters/
5. The Muse. (n.d.). How to use the STAR method to ace your job interview. The Muse. Retrieved from https://www.themuse.com/advice/star-interview-method
6. Indeed. (n.d.). 9 effective business networking tips for young professionals. Indeed Career Guide. Retrieved from https://in.indeed.com/career-advice/career-development/business-networking-tips
7. Dobroski, K. (2023, April 20). How to negotiate salary: 37 tips you need to know. The Muse. Retrieved from https://www.themuse.com/advice/how-to-negotiate-salary-37-tips-you-need-to-know
8. HR Future. (2023, May 5). Navigating new terrain: The gig economy's transformative influence on career paths. HR Future. Retrieved from https://www.hrfuture.net/future-of-work/gig-economy/navigating-new-terrain-the-gig-economys-transformative-influence-on-career-paths/
9. Carson, R. (2023, May 24). Ultimate guide to budgeting for young adults & teens. Forbes. Retrieved from https://www.forbes.com/sites/rcarson/2023/05/24/how-to-develop-a-positive-financial-mindset/
10. HyperJar. (n.d.). Money management: The ultimate guide to budgeting for young adults and teens. Retrieved from https://hyperjar.com/blog/money-management-ultimate-guide-to-budgeting-for-young-adults-and-teens
11. Benvenuto, J. (2022, December 5). The best expense tracker apps. The Balance. Retrieved from https://www.thebalancemoney.com/best-expense-tracker-apps-4158958
12. NerdWallet. (n.d.). The best budget apps for 2024. NerdWallet. Retrieved from https://www.nerdwallet.com/article/finance/best-budget-apps
13. FINRA. (n.d.). How your credit score impacts your financial future. FINRA. Retrieved from https://www.finra.org/investors/personal-finance/how-your-credit-score-impacts-your-financial-future

14. Equifax. (n.d.). Credit score ranges. Equifax. Retrieved from https://www.equifax.com/personal/education/credit/score/articles/-/learn/credit-score-ranges/
15. NerdWallet. (n.d.). How to read a credit report. NerdWallet. Retrieved from https://www.nerdwallet.com/article/finance/read-credit-report
16. Investopedia. (n.d.). How to improve your credit score fast. Investopedia. Retrieved from https://www.investopedia.com/how-to-improve-your-credit-score-4590097
17. Equifax. (n.d.). How to improve your credit score. Equifax. Retrieved from https://www.equifax.com/personal/education/credit/score/articles/-/learn/how-to-improve-credit-score/
18. Investopedia. (n.d.). Provisional income. In *Investopedia*. Retrieved from https://www.investopedia.com/terms/p/provisional-income.asp
19. Investopedia. (n.d.). Indexed universal life insurance. In *Investopedia*. Retrieved from https://www.investopedia.com/articles/insurance/09/indexed-universal-life-insurance.asp
20. NerdWallet. (n.d.). Indexed universal life insurance. Retrieved from https://www.nerdwallet.com/article/insurance/indexed-universal-life-insurance
21. Consumer Financial Protection Bureau. (n.d.). Tools and resources for adult financial education. Retrieved from https://www.consumerfinance.gov/consumer-tools/educator-tools/adult-financial-education/tools-and-resources/
22. Bougas, P. (2023, March 28). Best investments for young people. Investopedia. Retrieved from https://www.investopedia.com/articles/younginvestors/12/best-investments-for-young-people.asp
23. NerdWallet. (n.d.). Investment strategies. NerdWallet. Retrieved from https://www.nerdwallet.com/article/investing/investment-strategies
24. Investopedia. (n.d.). 5 common mistakes young investors make. Investopedia. Retrieved from https://www.investopedia.com/articles/younginvestors/09/common-mistakes-young-investors.asp
25. Investopedia. (n.d.). Taxes. In *Investopedia*. Retrieved from https://www.investopedia.com/taxes-4427724
26. Investopedia. (n.d.). Credit and debt. In *Investopedia*. Retrieved from https://www.investopedia.com/credit-and-debt-4689724
27. Investopedia. (n.d.). 529 plan. Retrieved from https://www.investopedia.com/terms/1/529plan.asp
28. Teen Vogue. (n.d.). How financial stress is impacting young people's mental health. Teen Vogue. Retrieved from https://www.teenvogue.com/story/how-financial-stress-is-impacting-young-peoples-mental-health
29. HelpGuide.org. (n.d.). Coping with financial stress. Retrieved from https://www.helpguide.org/articles/stress/coping-with-financial-stress.htm
30. Lindsey. (2024). How to set SMART financial goals + examples. Coping with Lindsey. Retrieved from https://copingwithlindsey.com/smart-financial-goals-examples/

31. Equifax. (n.d.). Why do people have credit card debt & how to avoid it. Equifax. Retrieved from https://www.equifax.com/personal/education/credit-cards/articles/-/learn/why-do-people-have-credit-card-debt/
32. U.S. National Library of Medicine. (n.d.). Exercise for mental health. PMC. Retrieved from https://www.ncbi.nlm.nih.gov/pmc/articles/PMC1470658/
33. Fay, M. (2016, April 26). Brain hack: How to make exercise a habit. Meghan Fay. Retrieved from https://www.meghanfay.com/blog/2016/brain-hack-make-exercise-habit
34. Sleep Foundation. (n.d.). Mental health and sleep. Sleep Foundation. Retrieved from https://www.sleepfoundation.org/mental-health
35. OnPlanners. (n.d.). Colorful weekly meal planner grocery list. Retrieved from https://onplanners.com/template/colorful-weekly-meal-planner-grocery-list
36. EatingWell. (n.d.). Healthy dinner recipes for beginner cooks. EatingWell. Retrieved from https://www.eatingwell.com/gallery/7577447/healthy-dinner-recipes-for-beginner-cooks/
37. Better Homes & Gardens. (n.d.). The ultimate home maintenance checklist for every season. Better Homes & Gardens. Retrieved from https://www.bhg.com/home-improvement/advice/home-maintenance-checklist/
38. Family Handyman. (n.d.). Home repairs you can do yourself. Family Handyman. Retrieved from https://www.familyhandyman.com/list/home-repairs-you-can-do-yourself/
39. University of Arkansas Division of Agriculture. (n.d.). Clean and green homemade cleaners. University of Arkansas System Division of Agriculture. Retrieved from https://www.uaex.uada.edu/environment-nature/water/quality/clean-green-homemade-cleaners.aspx
40. Verywell Mind. (n.d.). Active listening: Techniques, benefits, examples. Verywell Mind. Retrieved from https://www.verywellmind.com/what-is-active-listening-3024343
41. Verywell Health. (n.d.). How to set healthy boundaries with anyone. Verywell Health. Retrieved from https://www.verywellhealth.com/setting-boundaries-5208802
42. Psychology Today. (2022, August 8). 8 elements of a healthy relationship. Retrieved from https://www.psychologytoday.com/us/blog/invisible-bruises/202208/8-elements-healthy-relationship
43. Verywell Mind. (n.d.). Strengthening relationships. Retrieved from https://www.verywellmind.com/strengthening-relationships-4162997
44. Doe, S. (n.d.). The Eisenhower matrix: Organize tasks and boost productivity. Develop Good Habits. Retrieved from https://www.developgoodhabits.com/eisenhower-matrix/
45. Clear, J. (n.d.). How to be more productive by using the "Eisenhower box". James Clear. Retrieved from https://jamesclear.com/eisenhower-box
46. AppAdvice. (2016, September 8). Organize tasks by urgency and importance with Focus Matrix. Retrieved from https://appadvice.com/post/organize-tasks-by-urgency-and-importance-with-focus-matrix/717515
47. Medium. (n.d.). Boosting productivity with the Pomodoro Technique.

Medium. Retrieved from https://medium.com/@areebariaz/boosting-productivity-with-the-pomodoro-technique-my-success-story-eaafbc5e0b03

48. BetterUp. (n.d.). 10 best time management tools in 2023. BetterUp. Retrieved from https://www.betterup.com/blog/time-management-tools
49. Psychology Today. (2017, March). 11 ways to overcome procrastination. Psychology Today. Retrieved from https://www.psychologytoday.com/us/blog/better-than-perfect/201703/11-ways-to-overcome-procrastination
50. Impostor Syndrome Institute. (n.d.). How to overcome imposter syndrome - 10 steps. Impostor Syndrome Institute. Retrieved from https://impostorsyndrome.com/articles/10-steps-overcome-impostor/
51. MindTools. (n.d.). SMART goals: How to make your goals achievable. Retrieved from https://www.mindtools.com/pages/article/smart-goals.htm
52. Mindset Works. (n.d.). What is my mindset? Retrieved from https://www.mindsetworks.com/Science/Impact
53. Conaway, C. (n.d.). Seeking feedback with a pure intention. Cameron Conaway Blog. Retrieved from https://cameronconaway.com/blog/seeking-feedback-intention/
54. BetterUp. (n.d.). 7 ways to overcome fear of failure and move forward in life. BetterUp. Retrieved from https://www.betterup.com/blog/how-to-overcome-fear-of-failure

AUTHOR BIO

Arriving in the United States just as he was entering adulthood, Andyn faced many challenges and obstacles, from learning a new language, adapting to a new culture, and establishing financial independence. He started working as a paper delivery every morning from 4 am to 7 am, rain or shine, standing in assembly lines with summer jobs, and tutoring a disabled fellow friend during college. With an unwavering spirit and determination, he seized the opportunity to learn, adapt, and grow. His relentless efforts culminated in a B.S. degree in Engineering from UC Davis in Northern California, a testament to his perseverance.

Andyn's career has been a dynamic journey of service and personal growth. He began in the high-tech industry, working for renowned companies like AMD, Cypress, Micron, and Intel Corp in Silicon Valley, accumulating over 20 years of experience. However, driven by his passion for learning and personal growth, he made a bold transition into the financial industry. As a certified, licensed financial planner, he dedicated five years to helping others achieve their financial goals, a clear testament to his commitment to service and personal development.

Andyn's journey of service and personal growth continues as he now focuses on sharing his wealth of knowledge and experience through book publishing. His aim is to provide young adults with real-world life skills and insights. As a father of two young adults, he is acutely aware of today's youth's unique challenges and opportunities. His diverse background and relentless pursuit of excellence make him a unique and inspiring voice in the field, ready to guide and inspire the next generation.

Andyn's story is a testament to the power of resilience, continuous learning, and the pursuit of personal and professional growth.

www.ingramcontent.com/pod-product-compliance
Lightning Source LLC
LaVergne TN
LVHW011520200926
848484LV00001B/88

* 9 7 9 8 9 9 1 5 5 7 7 2 6 *